STRATEGIC BUSINESS MANAGEMENT
From planning to performance

CGMA

Chartered Global Management Accountant®

Powered by

AICPA® | CIMA

13379-359

Notice to Readers

Strategic Business Management: Planning to Performance does not represent an official position of the American Institute of Certified Public Accountants, and it is distributed with the understanding that the author and the publisher are not rendering legal, accounting, or other professional services in this publication. If legal advice or other expert assistance is required, the services of a competent professional should be sought.

1 2 3 4 5 6 7 8 9 0 PIP 1 9 8 7 6 5 4 3

ISBN: 978-1-93735-235-6

AUTHOR BIOGRAPHY

GARY COKINS, CPIM

Gary Cokins is an internationally recognised expert, speaker and author in advanced cost management and performance improvement systems. He is a Principal in Business Consulting involved with analytics and enterprise performance and risk management solutions with SAS, a leading provider of enterprise performance management and business analytics software headquartered in Cary, North Carolina. Mr Cokins received a BS degree with honours in Industrial Engineering/Operations Research from Cornell University in 1971. He received his MBA from Northwestern University's Kellogg School of Management in 1974.

Cokins began his career as a strategic planner with FMC's Link-Belt Division and then served as Financial Controller and Operations Manager. In 1981 he began his management consulting career first with Deloitte Consulting. Next with KPMG, Cokins was trained on ABC by Harvard Business School Professors Robert S. Kaplan and Robin Cooper. Prior to joining SAS, Cokins headed the National Cost Management Consulting Services for Electronic Data Systems (EDS).

Cokins was the lead author of the acclaimed *An ABC Manager's Primer* sponsored by the Institute of Management Accountants (IMA). He is also the author of:

- *Activity Based Cost Management: Making It Work*
- *Activity Based Cost Management: An Executive's Guide*
- *Activity Based Cost Management in Government*
- *Performance Management: Finding the Missing Pieces to Close the Intelligence Gap*
- *Performance Management: Integrating Strategy Execution, Methodologies, Risk, and Analytics*

Cokins participates and serves on committees including: The AICPA, CAM-I, the American Association of Accountants (AAA), the International Federation of Accountants (IFAC), the Supply Chain Council, and the Institute of Management Accountants (IMA).

He serves on board of advisors and regularly posts articles for www.kpilibrary.com, www.smartdatacollective.com, http://bigfatfinanceblog.com/, www.information-management.com, www.iianalytics.com, and www.informs.org.

Mr Cokins resides in Cary, North Carolina with his wife, Pam Tower. He has two stepdaughters, Jennifer and Kristin, and two grandsons, Conor and Brodie. He can be contacted at garyfarms@aol.com or gary.cokins@sas.com.

CONTENTS

PART 1: OVERVIEW OF ENTERPRISE PERFORMANCE MANAGEMENT   1

1 INTRODUCTION   3

     A Dilemma for Accountants   3

     Accountants' Problem of Denial   4

2 ENTERPRISE PERFORMANCE MANAGEMENT: MYTH OR REALITY?   5

     Executive Pain—A Major Force Creating Interest in
Performance Management   6

     What Is EPM?   7

     Is EPM a New Methodology?   7

     Clarifying What EPM Is Not   8

     What Has Caused Interest in EPM?   9

     The EPM Framework for Value Creation   10

     The EPM as a Continuous Flow   12

     A Car Analogy for EPM   13

     Where Does Managerial Accounting Fit In?   14

     EPM Unleashes the ROI From Information   15

     Management's Quest for a Complete Solution   17

PART 2: MANAGERIAL ACCOUNTING   21

3 DO ACCOUNTANTS LEAD OR MISLEAD?   23

     The Perils of Poor Navigation Equipment   23

     The Perils of Poor Managerial Accounting   24

     The Accountant as a Bad Navigator   24

4 A TAXONOMY OF ACCOUNTING AND COSTING METHODS   27

   Confusion About Accounting Methods   27

   A Historical Evolution of Managerial Accounting   29

   An Accounting Framework and Taxonomy   29

      Asking What? So What? Then What?   31

      Predictive Versus Descriptive Accounting   32

   Co-existing Cost Accounting Methods   33

5 MANAGERIAL ACCOUNTING DESIGN COMPLYING WITH THE CAUSALITY PRINCIPLE   35

   Removing the Blindfold With ABC/M   35

   Overhead Expenses Are Displacing Direct Expenses   36

   Impact of Diversity in Products, Service Lines, Channels and Customers   37

   Growing Discontent With Traditional Calculation of Costs   38

   Activities Are Expressed With Action Verbs   39

   Drivers Trigger the Workload Costs   41

   Strategic Versus Operational ABC/M   42

6 STRATEGIC COST MANAGEMENT FOR PRODUCT PROFITABILITY ANALYSIS   45

   ABC/M Is a Multi-Level Cost Re-assignment Network   45

   Drivers: Resource, Cost, Activity and Cost Object Drivers   48

   Business and Organisational Sustaining Costs   48

   The Two Views of Costs: The Assignment View Versus the Process View   49

      Vertical Axis   50

      Horizontal Axis   50

   How Does Activity-Based Costing Compute Better Accuracies?   51

Activity-Based Management Rapid Prototyping: Getting Quick and Accurate Results 53

Product Profitability Analysis 54

Two Alternative Equations for Costing Activities and Cost Objects 55

PART 3: STRATEGY MANAGEMENT 57

7 THE PROMISE AND PERILS OF THE BALANCED SCORECARD 59

What Is a Balanced Scorecard? 59

Balanced Scorecards Are Companions to Strategy Maps 60

Measurements Are More of a Social System Than a Technical One 62

Scorecard or Report Card? The Impact of Senior Management's Attitude 63

GPS Navigators for an Organisation 63

How Are Balanced Scorecards and Dashboards Different? 64

Scorecards and Dashboards Serve Different Purposes 65

Scorecards Link the Executives' Strategy to Operations and the Budget 68

Dashboards Move the Scorecard's Dials 68

Strategy Is More Than Performing Better 68

Getting Past the Speed Bumps 69

8 DESIGNING A STRATEGY MAP AND BALANCED SCORECARD 71

Eight Steps to Create a Strategy Map 71

Scorecards and Strategy Maps: The Enabler for EPM 76

PART 4: PLANNING, BUDGETING AND FORECASTING 79

9 PREDICTIVE ACCOUNTING AND BUDGETING WITH MARGINAL EXPENSE ANALYSIS 81

What Is the Purpose of Management Accounting? 81

What Types of Decisions Are Made With Managerial Accounting Information? 82

Rationalisation   82

Planning and Budgeting   83

Capital Expense Justification   83

Make Versus Buy, and General Outsourcing Decisions   83

Process and Productivity Improvement   84

Activity-Based Cost Management as a Foundation for Predictive Accounting   84

Major Clue: Capacity Only Exists as a Resource   85

Predictive Accounting Involves Marginal Expense Calculations   86

Decomposing the Information Flows Figure   88

Framework to Compare and Contrast Expense Estimating Methods   90

Predictive Costing Is Modelling   91

Debates About Costing Methods   91

10 WHAT'S BROKEN ABOUT BUDGETING?   95

The Evolutionary History of Budgets   96

A Sea Change in Accounting and Finance   98

The Financial Management Integrated Information Delivery Portal   99

11 PUT YOUR MONEY WHERE YOUR STRATEGY IS   101

A Budgeting Problem   101

Value Is Created From Projects and Initiatives, Not Strategic Objectives   103

Driver-Based Resource Capacity and Spending Planning   104

Including Risk Mitigation With a Risk Assessment Grid   105

Four Types of Budget Spending: Operational, Capital, Strategic and Risk   107

From a Static Annual Budget to Rolling Financial Forecasts   108

Managing Strategy Is Learnable   108

PART 5: INTEGRATING ENTERPRISE RISK MANAGEMENT AND ENTERPRISE PERFORMANCE MANAGEMENT 111

12 THE INTEGRATION OF ENTERPRISE RISK AND ENTERPRISE PERFORMANCE MANAGEMENT 113

How Do ERM and EPM Fit Together? 113

Is Risk an Opportunity or Hazard? 114

Problems Quantifying Risk and Its Consequences 114

Types of Risk Categories 115

Risk-Based EPM Framework 117

Risk Managers: Friend or Foe of Profit Growth? 118

Invulnerable Today but Aimless Tomorrow 119

PART 6: BUSINESS ANALYTICS FOR ACCOUNTING AND FINANCE 121

13 WHAT WILL BE THE NEXT NEW MANAGEMENT BREAKTHROUGH? 123

The History of Management Breakthroughs 123

Will Business Analytics Be the Next Breakthrough? 124

14 HOW DO BUSINESS INTELLIGENCE, BUSINESS ANALYTICS AND ENTERPRISE PERFORMANCE MANAGEMENT FIT TOGETHER? 127

The Relationship Between Business Intelligence, Business Analytics and Enterprise Performance Management 128

Overcoming Barriers 129

15 CFO TRENDS WITH ANALYTICS 131

Analytics as the Only Sustainable Competitive Advantage 131

Resistance to Change and Presumptions of Existing Capabilities 132

Evidence of Deficient Use of Business Analytics in Finance and Accounting 133

Sobering Indication of the Advances Still Needed by the CFO Function 134

Moving From Aspirations to Practice With Analytics 135

Customer Profitability Analysis to Take Actions 135

Rationalising and Validating Key Performance Indicators in a Strategy Map and Balanced Scorecard 136

Moving From Possibilities to Probabilities With Analytics 137

Fill in the Blanks: Which X Is Most Likely to Y? 139

Increased Employee Retention 139

Increased Customer Profitability 139

Increased Product Shelf Opportunity 139

The CFO Function Needs to Push the Envelope 140

PART 7: HOW TO BEGIN IMPLEMENTING ENTERPRISE PERFORMANCE MANAGEMENT 143

16 WHERE DO YOU BEGIN IMPLEMENTING ANALYTICS-BASED PERFORMANCE MANAGEMENT? 145

Accept That Analytics-Based EPM Is About Integration and Speed 145

Assuming an Enlightened Leadership Team, Then What? 146

Embrace Uncertainty With Predictive Analytics 147

17 A CALL TO ACTION—BUILDING A BUSINESS CASE 149

The Obsession With ROI Justifications 149

Management and the IT Function Can Be Obstacles 150

Is EPM Art, Craft or Science? 151

Balancing a Smart, as Well as a Healthy, Organization 151

The Power of Business Analytics 152

The Future of Analytics-Based EPM 152

FOREWORD

The past century has witnessed the rapid advance of financial accounting, an advance driven by the 20th century's development of new and more sophisticated business practices, concepts and theories and the increasing size, complexity and reach of organisations. Not only have accountants been able to develop new financial accounting tools and techniques to keep up with this ever more complex environment, they've been able to capitalise on the revolution in information technology and found ways to use technology to become more productive in their endeavours.

The tools and techniques used to measure where an organisation has been, however, are not the same as those it needs to navigate it toward its targeted destination. Because compliance with the financial accounting rules promulgated to regulate and control businesses in a complex economy are mandatory, accountants have spent the vast majority of their time and attention ensuring that historical results are reported in a manner that will keep their organisations 'in compliance.' Buried on the bottom of their to-do lists have been the optional areas of accounting that are not governed by regulators but are essential to the long-term success of a business, namely, (1) the provision of comprehensive and economically sound management information, (2) the creation of systems for using that information to support the formulation of an effective business strategy, and (3) the development of metrics to facilitate the execution of that strategy and generate the desired results. Although accountants have been focusing on the task of business compliance, they have been neglecting the support necessary for business success.

In this book, Gary Cokins shares his four decades of experience in cost and performance measurement and management to help accountants grow (as he puts it) 'from bean counters to bean growers.' Just as accountants are in a unique position to facilitate and coordinate the efforts of specialists within their organisations to reach organisational goals, Cokins is in a unique position to provide accountants with the tools needed to become more valuable resources to their organisations. Although not an accountant himself, Gary served as a controller for a major manufacturing organisation and has worked closely with accounting professionals in both academia and industry for over a quarter century. His experience, however, goes far beyond that. He has worked extensively with those professionals who require the guidance and tools he describes to effectively do their jobs, from supply chain managers to marketing executives and from CEOs to first-line operating managers. To top it off, his extensive experience as a speaker and writer on the topic have given him the communication skills to pass along his knowledge in an entertaining and understandable manner.

The 21st century is a tough time for senior managers. Customers increasingly view products and service lines as commodities and place pressure on prices as a result. Business mergers and employee layoffs are ongoing and, inevitably, there is a limit, which is forcing management to come to grips with truly managing their resources for maximum yield and internal organic sales growth. A company cannot forever cut costs to increase its prosperity.

It is imperative that financial executives at 21st century organisations provide management with comprehensive and sound decision support information, guide them in formulating an effective business strategy and provide them with means of linking that strategy to execution through an effective enterprise performance management system. That's what accounting executives need to be today—the financial arm of an organisation, adding value by providing it with the information it needs to thrive and grow in a worldwide, hyper-competitive business environment—not simply by 'doing budgets' and reporting results after the fact.

By incorporating the concepts and techniques described in Cokins' book, accountants truly can take on the mantle of management and grow far beyond the effective administrator role they are limited to in most organisations. If you're satisfied sitting in the stern of your organisation's ship measuring and studying its wake, the wisdom imparted in this book is not for you; but, if you want to take your place in the bow of the ship and help navigate it to a successful future, read on. You can—and should—make a real difference.

Douglas T. Hicks, CPA
Bloomfield Hills, Michigan
May 19, 2012

Douglas T. Hicks, CPA, has been a cost measurement and management consultant for over 27 years and is the author of *I May Be Wrong, But I Doubt It: How Accounting Information Undermines Profitability*.

Part 1

OVERVIEW OF ENTERPRISE PERFORMANCE MANAGEMENT

'Nothing else in the world...not all the armies...is so
powerful as an idea whose time has come.'
—Victor Hugo, *The Future of Man* (1861)

1

INTRODUCTION

The CFO finance and accounting function is evolving from its traditional role of collecting data, validating data and reporting information to a more value-adding role of supporting analysis for decision making. Progress has been notable. There is much written and discussed about how the CFO function's role should expand to one of being a strategic advisor to the executive team and an enabler for the workforce. However the upside potential is substantial.

Trends demonstrating progress include the shift from profitability reporting of products and standard service lines to the more encompassing view of customer profitability reporting using activity-based costing (ABC) principles. This is similar in industry to how suppliers often are viewed by customers as a commodity. In response, suppliers are expected to offer ideas and innovation to customers to differentiate themselves. Simply replace 'users' with 'customers' and 'suppliers' with 'accountants' in those last sentences. You will then understand what I mean. Accountants inevitably will need to embrace financial planning and analysis with enterprise performance management (EPM), which includes business analytics. To sum up, financial accounting is about valuation. In contrast, managerial accounting is about creating value. This means accountants need to expand from being bean counters or bean growers.

Another example of CFO function trends has been the development of strategy maps to report and monitor both financial and non-financial key performance indicators (KPIs). An additional example is a swing from traditional cost centre budgeting and variances control toward driver-based rolling financial forecasts using predictive analytics integrated across business processes. A third example is that enterprise risk management (ERM) is now being integrated with EPM, and the CFO function is increasingly involved with taking responsibility for ERM.

The opportunity is now for accountants to contribute more to improving organisational performance.

A DILEMMA FOR ACCOUNTANTS

The following is an edited excerpt from an e-mail sent to me from an accountant I have known for years.

> I left my job with Xxxxx in 2009. Most of the VPs there did not understand strategy execution or managerial accounting. A few others and I tried to spread the word for about two years. It was just always a struggle to get buy-in for strategy execution, a balanced scorecard, dashboards or driver-based budgeting and rolling financial forecasts. Our guys weren't really interested in profitability modelling or using any activity-based

costing. I tried to do one driver-based budgeting project, but their accounting software could not handle it. It is sad.

What can be said after reading his note? My intent is not to alienate some readers. I simply want to illustrate that the field of accounting will eventually need to deal with its denial problem.

The frustration with the lack of progress in managerial accounting is prevalent on Linkedin.com discussion groups related to accounting. The discussions exhibit annoyance bordering on infuriation caused by attempts to introduce progressive managerial accounting methods and practices that are rejected—or at least under-appreciated—by their organisation's managers and accounting colleagues.

ACCOUNTANTS' PROBLEM OF DENIAL

By denial, I mean the false belief that accounting's main purpose is what I just mentioned: to only collect, validate and report data. It is so much more. The accounting profession must shift its emphasis to embrace better and more robust methods of financial planning and analysis.

This book is intended to dispel misconceptions about impediments that block accountants from making progress. It is intended to provide an understanding about how various enterprise performance management methodologies work, can be integrated and can be imbedded with analytical techniques.

2

ENTERPRISE PERFORMANCE MANAGEMENT: MYTH OR REALITY?

Confusion exists in the marketplace about the term *performance management*. If you research the term, you will see what I mean.

The confusion begins with which type of performance management we are referring to. This confusion, in part, is due to semantics and language. We often see in the press the acronyms BPM for *business performance management*, CPM for *corporate performance management* and EPM for *enterprise performance management*. Just like the foreign language words *merci, gracias, danke shön* and *thank you* all mean the same thing, so do these acronyms. For this book, I choose to use *enterprise performance management* and its acronym EPM. I will also use analytics-based enterprise performance management when there is emphasis on analytics imbedded in the various EPM methodologies.

Additional confusion is that EPM is perceived by many as far too narrow. It is often referenced as a CFO initiative with a bunch of measurement dashboards for feedback. It is much, much more. More recent confusion comes from the term being narrowly applied to a single function or department, such as marketing performance management or information technology performance management.

The term *performance management* historically referred to individual employees and was used by personnel for employee appraisals. Today, it is widely accepted as enterprise performance management of an organisation as a whole, whether it is a commercial, not-for-profit or government organisation. The performance of employees is an important element to improve an organisation's performance, but in the broad framework of EPM, human capital management is just one component.

Most new improvement methodologies typically begin with misunderstandings about what they are and are not. Perhaps that is why the famous business management author, Peter Drucker, observed that it can take decades before a new and reliable management technique becomes widely adopted. Misunderstandings typically are not a result of ignorance but, rather, inexperience. So EPM is predictably laden with misconceptions due to the lack of experience with it. That is now changing.

A purpose of this book is to remove the confusion and clarify about what EPM really is, what it does and how to make it work. Let's begin with discussing a major reason why there is such high interest in EPM.

EXECUTIVE PAIN—A MAJOR FORCE CREATING INTEREST IN PERFORMANCE MANAGEMENT

It is a tough time for senior managers. Customers increasingly view products and service lines as commodities and place pressure on prices as a result. Business mergers and employee layoffs are continuing and, inevitably, there is a limit, which is forcing management to deal with truly managing their resources for maximum yield and internal organic sales growth. A company cannot forever cut costs to increase its prosperity. Evidence shows that it is also a tough time to be a chief executive. Surveys by the Chicago-based employee recruiting firm, Challenger, Gray & Christmas, Inc., repeatedly reveal increasing rates of involuntary job turnover at the executive level compared to a decade ago.[1] Boards of directors, no longer a ceremonial role, have become activists. Their impatience with CEOs failing to meet shareholder expectations of financial results is leading to job firings of CEOs, CFOs and executive team members.

In complex and overhead-intensive organisations in which constant re-direction to a changing landscape is essential, the main cause for executive job turnover is the failure to implement their strategy. There is a big difference between formulating a strategy and implementing it. What is the answer for executives who need to expand their focus beyond cost control and toward sustained economic value creation for shareholders and other, more long-term strategic directives? EPM provides managers and employee teams at all levels with the capability to directly move toward their defined strategies.

One cause for failures in strategy implementation is that managers and employee teams typically have no clue about what their organisation's strategy is. Most employees, if asked, cannot articulate their executive team's organisation strategy. The implication of this is significant. If managers and employee teams do not understand their organisation's strategic objectives, then how can the executives expect employees to know how what they do each week or month contributes to the achievement of the executive's strategy? That is, employees effectively can implement a strategy only when they clearly understand the strategy and how they contribute to its achievement. The balanced scorecard has been heralded as an effective tool for the executive team to communicate and cascade their strategy down through their managers and employees to improve strategy attainment.

A balanced scorecard is designed to align the work and priorities of employees with the strategic objectives that comprise an organisation's defined mission. However there is confusion with this methodology. Many organisations claim to have a balanced scorecard, but there is little consensus about what it is. Worse yet, very few have designed a strategy map for which the scorecard and its key performance indicators (KPIs) are intended to be derived from as its companion. The strategy map is orders of magnitude more important than the scorecard itself—the latter of which should be viewed more as merely a feedback mechanism.

Even with the presence of a strategy map and its balanced scorecard with visual at-a-glance dashboards that display KPIs, are they enough? Or do they only provide one component of delivering economic value creation through achieving the strategy?

An organisation's interest ultimately is not just to monitor scorecard and dashboard dials of measures but, more importantly, to move those dials. That is, reporting historical performance information is a minimum requirement for managing performance. Scorecards and dashboards generate questions. But beyond answering 'what happened?' organisations need to know 'why did it happen?' and going forward 'what could happen?' and ultimately 'what is the best choice of my options?'

WHAT IS EPM?

EPM is all about improvement—synchronising improvement to create value for and from customers with the result of economic value creation to shareholders and owners. The scope of EPM obviously is very broad, which is why EPM must be viewed at an enterprise-wide level.

A simple definition of EPM[2] is 'the translation of plans into results—execution.' It is the process of managing an organisation's strategy. For commercial companies, strategy can be reduced to three major choices:[3]

- What products or service lines should we offer?
- What markets and types of customers should we serve?
- How are we going to win—and keep winning?

Although EPM provides insights to improve all three choices, its power is in achieving choice number three—winning by continuously adjusting and successfully implementing strategies. EPM does this by helping managers to sense earlier and more quickly and effectively respond to uncertain changes.

Why is responding to changes so critical? External forces are producing unprecedented uncertainty and volatility. Examples include changes in consumer preferences, foreign currency exchange rates and commodity prices. The Internet, global communications, social networks, relaxation of international trade barriers and political upheavals have also introduced vibrations and turbulence. The speed of change makes calendar-based planning and long cycle-time planning with multi-year horizons unsuitable for managing. As a result, strategies are never static but, rather, they are dynamic. Executives constantly must adjust them based on external forces and new opportunities. Strategies and operational plans are never perfect. Imagine if employees at all levels—from the executives to front-line workers—could answer these questions every day:

- What if my plan or decision is wrong?
- What are the consequences if I am wrong?
- If I'm wrong, what can I do about it?

EPM helps answer those questions. EPM can be summed up by stating that it gives an organisation the capability to quickly anticipate, react and respond. If executives were given the choice between two scenarios, one with relatively more precise information for the next three months with relatively less precision and more uncertainty for the next two years, and the other choice the opposite, I believe most executives would select the first one. EPM helps anticipate problems earlier in the time-cycle.

IS EPM A NEW METHODOLOGY?

Some good news is that EPM is not a new methodology that everyone now has to learn but, rather, EPM tightly integrates business improvement and analytic methodologies that executives and employee teams are already familiar with. Think of EPM as an umbrella concept. EPM integrates operational and financial information into a single decision-support and planning framework. These include strategy mapping, balanced scorecards, costing (including activity-based cost management), budgeting, forecasting and resource capacity requirements planning. These methodologies fuel other core solutions, such as customer relationship management (CRM), supply chain management, risk management, and human capital management systems, as well as lean management and other initiatives such as the Six Sigma business management strategy. It is quite a stew, but they all blend together.

EPM increases in power the greater these managerial methodologies are integrated and unified with all types of analytics—particularly predictive analytics. Predictive analytics are important because organisations are shifting from managing by control and reacting to after-the-fact data toward managing with anticipatory planning so they can be proactive and make adjustments before problems occur. Unfortunately, at most organisations, EPM's portfolio of methodologies typically are implemented or operated in a silo-like sequence and in isolation of each other. It is as if the project teams and managers responsible for each methodology live in parallel universes. We all know there are linkages and interdependencies, so we know they should all somehow be integrated. However, these components are like pieces of a jigsaw puzzle that everyone knows somehow fits together, but the picture on the puzzle's box cover is missing.

EPM both technologically and socially provides that picture of integration. EPM makes implementing the strategy everyone's top job—it makes employees behave like they are the business owners. It is the integration of the methodologies paired with analytics that is the key to completing the full vision of the EPM framework.

CLARIFYING WHAT EPM IS NOT

As earlier mentioned, EPM is sometimes confused as a personnel system for individual employees. It is much more encompassing. EPM embraces the methodologies, measurements, processes, software tools and systems that manage the performance of an organisation as a whole. Also, EPM should not be confused with the more mechanical *business process management* tools that automate the creating, revising, and operating of workflow processes, such as for a customer order entry and its accounts receivable system. Also, EPM is not just performance measurement. Measurements and indicators simply are a piece of the broad EPM framework.

To minimise confusion, there is no single EPM methodology because EPM spans the complete management planning and control cycle. Hence, EPM is not a process or a system. Substantial interdependencies exist among multiple improvement methodologies and systems. In a sense, everything is connected, and changes in one area can affect performance elsewhere. For example, you cannot separate cost management from performance because increases or decreases in expense funding generally affects performance results. For EPM to be accepted as the overarching integrator of methodologies, it must answer the question will EPM prove to be a value multiplier?

Think of EPM as a broad, end-to-end union of integrated methodologies and solutions with four major purposes: collecting data, transforming and modelling the data into information, analysing the information and Web-reporting it to users and decision makers. EPM is also not software, but software is an essential enabling technology for any organisation to achieve the full vision of the EPM framework. I view EPM as overarching from the C-level executives cascading down through the organisation and the processes it performs. EPM is all the way from the top desk to the desk top.

Primitive forms of EPM existed decades ago. These forms were present before EPM was given a formal label by the IT research firms and software vendors. EPM arguably existed before there were computers. In the past, organisations made decisions based on knowledge, experience, or intuition. As time passed, the margin for error grew slimmer. Computers reversed this problem by creating lots of data storage memory, but this led organisations to complain they were drowning in data but starving for information—thus, distinguishing the word *information* as the transformation of raw data, usually transactional data, into a more useful form. In the 1990s, with the speed up of integration with computer technology, both at a technical level of data base management and at a business level of user-friendly software applications for all employees, the term EPM took root.

WHAT HAS CAUSED INTEREST IN EPM?

As earlier mentioned, ambiguity and confusion exists about what EPM really is. Regardless of how one defines or describes it, what is arguably more useful is to understand what EPM does and what business forces have created executive's interest in having it.

There have been, in my opinion, eight major forces that have caused interest in performance management because it resolves these seven problems:

1. *Failure to implement the strategy.* Although executive teams typically can formulate a good strategy, their major frustration has been failure to implement it. The increasing rate of involuntary job turnover of CEOs is evidence of this problem. A major reason for this failure is that most managers and employees cannot explain their organisation's strategy, so they really do not know how their weekly or monthly duties contribute to their executives' tactical intent. Strategy maps, balanced scorecards, key performance indicators (KPIs) and dashboards are some of the components of EPM's suite of solutions that address this.

2. *Unfulfilled return on investment (ROI) promises from transactional systems.* Few, if any, organisations believe they actually realised the expected ROI promised by their software vendor that initially justified their large-scale IT investment in major systems (eg, CRM, enterprise resource planning [ERP]). The CIO has been increasingly criticised for expensive technology investments that, although probably necessary to pursue, have fallen short of their planned results and ROI. The executive management team is growing impatient with information technology investments. EPM is a value multiplier that unleashes the power and ROI payback from the raw data produced by these operating systems. EPM's analytics increase the leverage of CRM, ERP and other core transactional systems.

3. *Escalation in accountability for results with consequences.* Accelerating change that requires quick decisions at all levels is resulting in a shift from a command-and-control managerial style to one in which managers and employees are empowered. A major trend is for executives to communicate their strategy to their workforce, be assured the workforce understands it and is funded to take actions and to then hold those managers and employee teams accountable. Unlike our parents, who stayed at their workplaces for decades until they retired, today, there is no place to hide in an organisation anymore. Accountability is escalating, but it has no authority without having consequences. EPM adds authority and traction by integrating KPIs from the strategy map-derived scorecard with employee compensation reward and motivation systems.

4. *The need for quick trade-off decision analysis.* Decisions must now be made much more rapidly. Unlike in the past when organisations could test and learn or have endless briefing meetings with their upper management, today, an employee often must quickly make a decision. This means employees must understand their executive team's strategy. In addition, internal tension and conflict are natural in all organisations. Most managers know that decisions they make that help their own function may

adversely affect others. They just don't know who is negatively affected or by how much. A predictive impact of decision outcomes using analytics is essential. EPM provides analytical tools, including regression and correlation analysis. Insights gained range from marginal cost analysis to what-if scenario simulations that support resource capacity analysis and future profit margin estimates.

5. *Mistrust of the managerial accounting system.* Managers and employees are aware that the accountants' arcane 'cost allocation' practices using non-causal, broad-brushed averaging factors (eg, input labour hours, % of sales) to allocate non-product-related, indirect and shared expenses result in flawed and misleading profit and cost reporting. Some cynically refer to them as the 'mis-allocation' system. Consequently, they do not know where money is made or lost or what drives their costs. EPM embraces techniques like activity-based costing to increase cost accuracy and reveal and explain what drives the so-called 'hidden costs of overhead'—the indirect and shared expenses. It provides cost transparency and visibility that organisations desire but often cannot get from their accountants' traditional internal management accounting system.

6. *Poor customer value management.* Everyone now accepts how critical it is to satisfy customers to grow a business. However it is more costly to acquire a new customer than to retain an existing one. In addition, products and standard service lines in all industries have become commodity-like. Mass selling and advertising are obsolete concepts. This shifts the focus to require a much better understanding of channel and customer behaviour and costs to serve. This type of understanding is needed to know which types of existing customers and new sales prospects to grow, retain, acquire or win back using differentiated service levels—and how much to optimally spend on each type of customer that is worth pursuing. It requires working backwards by knowing each customer's unique preferences. EPM includes sales and marketing analytics for various types of customer segmentations to better understand where to focus the sales and marketing budget for maximum yield and financial payback. *Return on customer* is an emerging term.

7. *Dysfunctional supply chain management.* Most organisations now realise it is no longer sufficient for their own organisation to be agile, lean and efficient. They are now co-dependent on their trading partners, both upstream and downstream, to also be agile, lean and efficient. To the degree their partners are not, then waste and extra unnecessary costs enters the end-to-end value chain. These costs ultimately pass along the chain, resulting in higher prices to the end consumer, which can reduce sales for all of the trading partners. Sadly, there have been centuries of adversarial relationships between buyers and sellers. EPM addresses these issues with powerful forecasting tools, increasing real-time decisions and financial transparency across the value chain. It allows trading partners to collaborate to join in mutually beneficial projects and joint process improvements.

THE EPM FRAMEWORK FOR VALUE CREATION

One of the most ambiguous terms in discussions about business and government is *value*. Everybody wants value in return for whatever they exchanged to get value. Whose value is more important, and who is entitled to claiming it? Customers conclude that they receive value if the benefits they received from a product or service meets or exceeds what they paid for it (including time, investment, cost, etc). However shareholders and stakeholders believe if their investment return is less than the economic return they could have received from equally or less risky investments (eg, a UK gilt or US Treasury bill), then they are disappointed. Value to employees is another issue altogether, usually tied to compensation and job satisfaction.

Three groups believe they are entitled to value: customers, shareholders and stakeholders and employees. Are they rivals? What are the trade-offs? Is there an invisible hand controlling checks and balances to maintain an economic equilibrium so that each group gets its fair share? Are some groups more entitled to receiving value than others?

Figure 2-1 illustrates the interdependent methodologies that comprise EPM for a commercial organisation. Before I describe how the figure represents EPM, first just look at this figure and ask yourself what box in the figure has the most important words? What box has the answer? It depends on who you are in the organisation.

Figure 2-1: EPM is Circulatory and Simultaneous
Shareholder wealth creation is not a goal. It is a result.

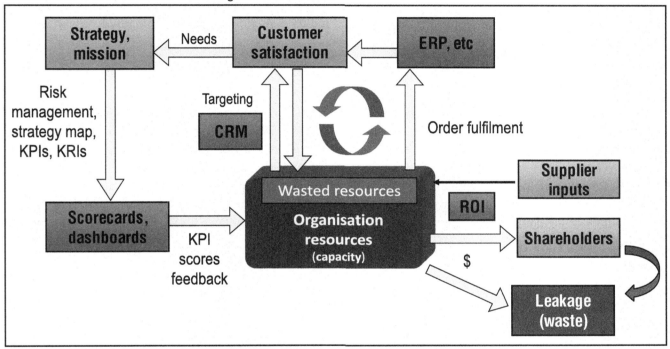

Source: Copyright Gary Cokins. Used with permission.

If you are the CEO and executive team, the answer must be the 'Mission and Strategy' box. That is the CEO's primary job: to define and constantly adjust organisational strategy as the environment changes. (Their secondary job is to grow employee competencies and hire exceptional talent.) Strategy formulation is why CEOs are paid high salaries and reside in large, corner offices. However, after the strategy definition is complete and maintained through adjustments to be current, then the core business processes take over, with competent process owners held accountable to manage and improve each process.

You, as a reader, might probably have answered that 'Customer Satisfaction' is the most important box in the figure. With businesses' increasing focus on customer, many will agree with you. Customer satisfaction and loyalty encompasses four customer-facing trends:

1. *Customer retention.* Recognising that it is relatively more expensive to acquire a new customer than to retain an existing one.

2. *Source of competitive advantage.* Gaining an edge by shifting from commodity-like product differentiation to value-adding service differentiation apart from products or standard service lines.

3. *Micro-segmenting of customers.* With a focus on customers' unique preferences rather than mass selling. Mass marketing days are nearing an end.

4. *The Internet.* The Internet is shifting power irreversibly from suppliers to customers and buyers.

It's easy to conclude that a customer focus is critical.

To explain Figure 2-1, first focus on the three counter-clockwise arrows at the centre of the figure, starting and ending with the 'Customer Satisfaction' box. The two thick arrows represent the primary universal core business processes possessed by any organisation, regardless of whether they are in the commercial or public sector: Take an order or assignment and fulfil that order or assignment. These two processes apply to any organisation. Orders, assignments or tasks are received, and then organisations attempt to implement them. Order fulfilment is the most primary and universal core process of any organisation. An example in health care is a hospital admitting patients and then treating them. The IT support systems needed to fulfil these two core processes, represented by the two thick arrows, are typically called *front office* and *back office* systems. This is the realm of 'better, faster and cheaper.'

The customer-facing, front office systems include customer intelligence and CRM systems. This is also where targeting customers, marketing campaigns, sales processes and work order management systems reside. The back office systems are where the fulfilment of customer or work orders and sales process planning and operations reside—the world of ERP and lean management and Six Sigma quality initiatives. The output from this process planning and implementation box is the delivered product or service intended to meet the customer needs. To the degree that customer turnover exceeds all of an organisation's expenses, including the cost of capital, then profit (and positive free cash flow) eventually accumulates into the shareholder's box in the figure's lower right.

THE EPM AS A CONTINUOUS FLOW

Figure 2-1 should be viewed as a circulatory flow of information and resource consumption similar to your body's heart and blood vessel system. As earlier mentioned, an organisation's EPM practices have been around for decades, even before computers. Think of how speeding the flow and widening constrictions will increase throughput velocity and the yield from the organisation's resources. *More with less. Value for money.* These are the terms associated with EPM.

Figure 2-1 is dynamic. The starting point of the diagram begins with the 'Customer Satisfaction' box. The need to satisfy customers and make them more loyal is the major input into senior management's box in the figure's upper left: 'Mission and Strategy.' As the executive team adjusts their organisation's formulated strategy, they continuously communicate it to employees with their strategy map and its companion balanced scorecard. With strategic objective adjustments, they may abandon some KPIs intended to align work behaviour with the outdated strategy. In those cases, KPIs associated with outdated plans are not unimportant but, rather, now less important. The abandoned KPIs become performance indicators in operational dashboards. The team may also add new KPIs or adjust the KPI weightings for various employee teams. As the feedback is received from the scorecards and dashboards, all employees can answer the key question 'How am I doing on what is important?' The power of that question is in its second half, what is most important. The selection of good

KPIs is critical. With analysis for causality, corrective actions can then occur. Note in the figure that the output from scorecards and dashboards does not stop at the organisation's boundary, but it penetrates all the way through to influence the employee behaviour—the increasingly important intangible assets. This, in turn, leads to better implementation.

Enterprise risk management (ERM) is included in the 'Mission and Strategy' box. Risks are assessed, and key risk indicators are identified and monitored.

Continuing on, the organisation's marketing and sales can better target which existing and potentially new customers to retain, grow, acquire and win back—and the optimal amount to spend on each one with differentiated service levels, deals, discounts or offers.

Finally, there is the order fulfilment loop. Take customer orders and efficiently fulfil the orders.

As this circulatory system is streamlined and digitised with better information, decisions and more focused and aligned employee work, the result is a faster and higher yield of shareholder wealth creation. Remember, shareholder wealth creation is not a goal—it is a result. It is the result of addressing all the methodologies in the flow. In the end, when EPM is integrated with ERM, then the figure is more broadly about 'better, faster cheaper … and smarter and safer.' The 'smarter' comes not only from process improvements but from facilitating the executive team's strategic objectives. The 'safer' comes from ERM.

Where is the box for innovation in Figure 2-1? It is not there because it arguably must be inside every box and arrow in the diagram. Innovation is as mission-critical today as achieving quality was in the 1980s. It is assumed to be a given—an entry ticket to even compete. I do not dwell on innovation in this book because I believe it, and its associated breakthrough thinking, is so critical that I leave it to other authors to devote entire books on this most important topic.

The best executive teams do not consider any of the components in this figure as optional—they are all essential. The best executive teams, however, not only know the priorities of where in the flow to place emphasis to widen constrictions but also where to improve all the other methodologies in the flow. Improvements may come from rapid prototyping and iterative re-modelling to learn things previously unknown and that will evolve into permanent and repeatable production reporting and decision support systems. The key is to integrate the EPM methodologies because much can be learned from addressing the lower priorities, such as by implementing a higher level activity-based costing model for customer segment profitability reporting. These quick-start approaches reveal findings that can contribute to altering strategic objectives formulated in the beginning of the circulatory flow.

A CAR ANALOGY FOR EPM

As mentioned, all organisations have been performing EPM well before it was labelled as such. It can be argued that on the date all organisations were first created, they immediately were managing (or attempting to manage) their enterprise performance by offering products or services and fulfilling sales orders with some sort of strategy.

Imagine Figure 2-1 as an organisation being a poorly tuned car. Include in your imagination cogs in the engine, where some of the gear teeth are broken, some of the gears have moved apart and are disengaged, some of the gears are made of wood and are crumbling, and where someone threw sand in the gears. Further, imagine unbalanced tires, severe shimmy in the steering wheel, poor timing of engine pistons, thick power steering fluid and mucky oil in the crankcase. These collectively represent unstable, imbalanced and poorly operating methodologies of the EPM framework. Take that mental picture and conclude that any physical system of moving parts with tremendous vibration and part-wearing friction dissipates energy, wasting fuel and power. The car's fuel efficiency in miles per gallon or kilometres per litre would be low.

Now substitute the analogy of fuel efficiency with the rate of profits and shareholder wealth creation. At an organisational level, the energy dissipation from vibration and friction with lower fuel efficiency translates into wasted expenses where the greater the waste, then the lower the rate of shareholder wealth creation, and possibly wealth destruction. In a different case, you may find a car that seems perfect in every way in the mind of the customer, but it is not priced to make a profit, making the shareholders unhappy. In another case, the focus may be on producing a car at the lowest cost to the point of undermining customer satisfaction.

Now, replace that vision and imagine that same car with an engine with finely cut high-grade titanium cogs spinning at faster revolutions per minute. Imagine its tires finely balanced and its moving parts are well-lubricated and digitised with internal communications. The EPM framework (ie, the car) remains unchanged, but shareholders' wealth is more rapidly created because there is balance in quality, price and value to all. No vibration or friction. The higher fuel efficiency translates into a higher rate of shareholder wealth creation. That is how good EPM integrates the multiple methodologies of the EPM portfolio of components and provides better analysis and decision making that aligns work behaviour and priorities with the strategy. Strategic objectives are attained, and the consequence is relatively greater shareholder wealth creation.

One can take this analogy further with the strategy map and its derived target measures serving as the car's risk-mitigating global positioning system or GPS. When you are driving with a GPS instrument and you make a wrong turn, the GPS chimes in to tell you that you are off track, and it then provides you with a corrective action instruction. However, with most organisations' calendar-based and long cycle-time reporting, there is delayed reaction. The EPM framework includes a GPS.

WHERE DOES MANAGERIAL ACCOUNTING FIT IN?

Note that managerial accounting does not appear in Figure 2-1. That is because the output of a managerial accounting system is always the input to some place where decisions are made. The primary purpose of managerial accounting is for discovery—to ask better questions. In the figure, it supports every box and arrow in the diagram.

Managerial accounting (including activity-based cost management [ABC/M] data) is a key component in EPM. Its information permeates every single element in this scenario to help re-balance these sometimes competing values. By including managerial accounting as a foundational component to the EPM framework, we involve the language of money to support decision making and build better business cases.

Managerial accounting itself is not an improvement programme or execution system, like several other systems in the figure. Information from managerial accounting, such as from ABC/M, serves as an enabler for these systems. It supports better decision making. For example, ABC/M links customer value management (as determined by CRM systems) to shareholder value creation, which is heralded as essential for economic value management. The tug-of-war between CRM and shareholder wealth creation is the trade-off of excessively adding more value for customers at the risk of reducing wealth to shareholders.

Businesses ultimately will discover that customer value management, accomplished by targeting the marketing spend to different customer micro-segments, is the independent variable in the economic value equation. This equation then solves for the dependent variable for which the executive team is accountable to the governing board: shareholder wealth creation. EPM provides the framework to model this all-important relationship.

Is my figure the best diagram to represent the EPM framework? I do not know. Professional societies, management consultants and software vendors have their own diagrams. The key point is that EPM is not the narrow definition of being dashboards with better budgeting and financial reporting. EPM clearly is much broader and balances competing values.

EPM UNLEASHES THE ROI FROM INFORMATION

There is a shift in the source when organisations realise their financial ROI from tangible assets to the intangible assets of employee knowledge and information. That is, the shift is from spending on equipment, computer hardware and the like to knowledgeable workers applying information for decision making.

Figure 2-2 displays across the horizontal axis the stages that raw, transactional data passes through to become the knowledge, wisdom and intelligence to make better decisions that successful organisations will eventually experience. The vertical axis measures the power and ROI from transforming that data and leveraging it for realised results. The ROI exponentially increases from left to right.

Figure 2-2: The Intelligence Hierachy

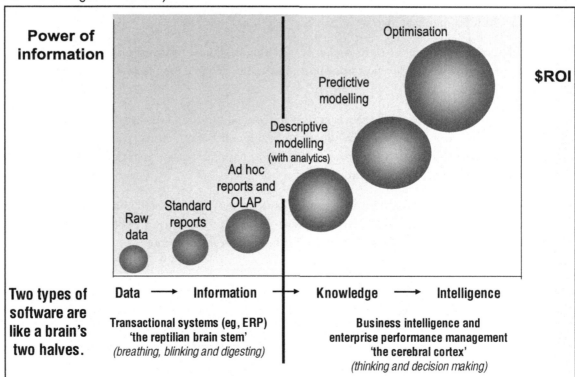

Source: Copyright Gary Cokins. Used with permission.

The three bubbles on the left side are the location of transactional data for daily operations and reporting. The three bubbles to the right are where the EPM framework of methodologies lifts the ROI. EPM included business intelligence (BI) and analytical software of all types.

Most organisations are mired in the lower left corner's first two bubbles, hostage to raw data and standard reports. When the feared year 2000 Y2K meltdown approached, many organisations replaced their home-grown software applications with commercial transactional ERP and CRM software. In some organisations, the CIO and IT staff allowed some managers to use basic query and reporting, online analytical processing tools to drill down to examine some of that data. However, this data restricts and confines workers to only know what happened in the past.

The power of BI, EPM and business analytics begins with the fourth bubble—descriptive modelling with analytics. As an example, ABC/M models the conversion of expense spending into the calculated costs of processes, work activities and the types of outputs, products, service lines, channels and customers that consumes an organisation's capacity. Costing is modelling. As another example, a strategy map and its associated scorecard and dashboard performance indicators is a model of how an organisation defines its linked strategic objectives and plans to achieve them. Data has been transformed into information. At this stage, employees can now know not just what happened but also why did it happen.

The fifth bubble passes from historical information, from which organisations are reactive, to predictive information, such as what-if scenarios and rolling financial forecasts, from which organisations are proactive. As earlier mentioned, organisations are shifting their management style from after-the-fact control based on examining variance deviations from plans, budgets and expectations to an anticipatory management style in which they can adjust spending and capacity levels as well as projects and initiative before changes in work demands arrive. Information is used for knowledge. At this stage, employees can now know not just what happened and why did it happen but also what can happen next.

The sixth and final bubble in the upper right corner is the highest stage—optimisation. At this point, organisations can select from all its decision options examined in the prior stage and answer which is the best decision and action to take.

IT transactional systems may be good at reporting past outcomes, but they fall short on being predictive for effective planning. Given a sound strategy, how does the organisation know if its strategy is achievable? What if pursuing the strategy and its required new programmes will cause negative cash flow or financial losses? Will resource requirements exceed the existing capacity?

Figure 2-2 is not intended to imply that the transactional software vendors of ERP or CRM are not with value. In fact, it is just the opposite. These vendors are excellent—at what their computer code is architected and designed to do. The real ROI lift comes from applying information in the context of gaining insights, solving problems and driving the implementation of strategy.

To simplify an understanding of computer software, it comes in two broad types—transactional and decision support. The latter type includes business intelligence, business analytics and EPM. These two types can be thought of similar to two broad components of the human brain. In the back of one's head, above the backbone spine, is the reptilian brain stem, evolved from early stages of life. It controls the most basic elements of life such as breathing, eye blinking, digesting food and sleeping. In the front of one's brain is the cerebral cortex, from which thinking, learning and decision making occurs.

The transactional software represented on in the left side of Figure 2-2 is essential. One must have it operating well. The better its condition, the better the BI, EPM and analytical software can leverage it. The real power and lift of ROI comes from the right side of Figure 2-2. The ROI lift from the analytics-based EPM framework illustrated in the figure demonstrates that the upside potential is enormous. Its purpose is to robustly analyse and understand one's own organisation, its customers, suppliers, markets, competitors and other external factors, from government regulators to the weather.

MANAGEMENT'S QUEST FOR A COMPLETE SOLUTION

Many organisations jump from improvement programme to programme, hoping that each new one may provide that big, yet elusive competitive edge, like a magic pill. However, most managers would acknowledge that pulling one lever for improvement rarely results in a substantial change—particularly a long-term, sustained change. The key for improving is integrating and balancing multiple improvement methodologies and integrating them with analytics of all types—particularly predictive analytics. In the end, organisations need top-down guidance with bottom-up execution.

Operating managers and employee teams toil daily, making choices involving natural tension, conflicts and trade-offs within their organisation. An example is how to improve customer service levels and cost-saving process efficiencies while restricted to fixed, contract-like budget constraints and profit targets. For example, a classic conflict in physical, product-based companies is that the sales force wants a lot of inventories to prevent missed sales opportunities from stock-out shortages. In contrast, the production folks want low, in-process and finished goods inventories so that they can apply the more proven, just-in-time production methods, rather than continue with the less effective batch-and-queue production methods of the 1980s.

Organisations that are enlightened enough to recognise the importance and value of their data often have difficulty in actually *realising* that value. Their data is often disconnected, inconsistent and inaccessible, resulting from too many non-integrated, single-point solutions. They have valuable, untapped data that is hidden in the reams of transactional data they collect daily. It is the syndrome of drowning in data, but starving for information.

How does EPM create more value lift? One fundamental thing EPM does is transforms transactional data into decision-support information. For example, employee teams struggle with questions like 'How do we increase customer service levels without increasing our budget?' or, 'Should we increase our field distribution warehouse space by 25% or instead have our trucks ship direct from our central warehouse?' How can employees answer these questions from examining transaction data from a payroll, procurement, general ledger accounting or ERP system? They cannot. Those systems were designed for a different purpose—short-term operating and control with historical reporting of what happened.

Unlocking the intelligence trapped in mountains of data has been, until recently, a relatively difficult task to effectively accomplish. EPM is a value multiplier to the substantial investment organisations have made in their transactional ERP and CRM software systems and technology but are often viewed as falling short of their expected ROI.

Fortunately, innovation in data storage technology is now significantly outpacing progress in computer processing, power-heralding a new era in which creating vast pools of digital data is becoming the preferred solution. As a result, there are now superior software tools that offer a complete suite of analytic applications and data models that enable organisations to tap into the virtual treasure trove of information they already possess and enable effective EPM on a huge scale that is enterprise-wide in scope. EPM is the integration of these technologies and methodologies. The EPM solutions suite provides the mechanism to bridge the business intelligence gap between the CEO's vision and employees' actions.

Endnotes

1 Webber, Alan; 'CEO bashing has gone too far;' *USA Today*, June 3, 2003, p. 15A.

2 There are several variants of enterprise performance management (EPM), including business performance management (BPM) and corporate performance management (CPM). Consider these other terms synonymous with EPM.

3 Brache, Alan. *How Organizations Work*. John Wiley & Sons, 2002; page 10.

Part 2

MANAGERIAL ACCOUNTING

'It is a common criticism of cost accountants that they spend too much time in working out elaborate distributions of expenses which are unimportant in themselves and which do not permit of an accurate distribution. Undoubtedly some of that criticism is deserved, but it should also be remembered that once the basis for distribution has been worked out, it can generally continue in use for some time.'
—H. G. Crockett, 'Some Problems in the Actual Installation of Cost Systems,' *National Association of Cost Accountants (NACA) Bulletin*, vol. 1, no. 8 (February 1921)

'Today the cost department of the average business is looked on as a right arm of first Importance in management. Without the cost department today 90 percent of our business would be out of existence...the cost department of the future is going to have more effect on the business and on the general management of business than any other single department...and, gentlemen, in my opinion the major portion of the work of the cost department of the future is going to be applying recognized principles of cost analysis to sales expenses, for there is the greatest evil in present-day industry—the high cost, extravagant, outrageous cost, of distribution.'
—James H. Rand, President
Remington Rand Company, 1921

3

DO ACCOUNTANTS LEAD OR MISLEAD?

Over the past few years I have continually discussed a paradox with Doug Hicks, President of D.T. Hicks & Co., a performance improvement consulting firm in Farmington Hills, Michigan. The paradox, which continues to puzzle me, is how CFOs and controllers can be aware that their managerial accounting data is flawed and misleading yet not take action to do anything about it.

Now, I'm not referring to the financial accounting data used for external reporting. That information passes strict audits. I'm referring to the managerial accounting internally used for analysis and decisions. For this data, there is no governmental regulatory agency enforcing rules, so the CFO can apply any accounting practice he or she likes. For example, the CFO may choose to allocate substantial indirect expenses for product and standard service line costs based on broadly averaged allocation factors, such as number of employees or sales dollars. The vast differences among products mean each product is unique in its consumption of expenses throughout various business processes and departments, with no relation to the arbitrary cost factor chosen by the CFO. By not tracing those indirect costs to outputs based on true cause and effect relationships—referred to as *drivers*—some product costs become undervalued and others overvalued. It is a zero-sum error situation.

THE PERILS OF POOR NAVIGATION EQUIPMENT

I speculated to Doug that I think some CFOs and controllers are simply lazy. They do not want to do any extra work. Doug explained this counterintuitive phenomenon using a fable:

Imagine that several centuries ago there was a navigator who served on a wooden sailing ship that regularly sailed through dangerous waters. It was the navigator's job to make sure the captain always knew where the ship had been, where she was and how to safely and efficiently move the ship from one point to another. In the performance of his duties, the navigator relied on a set of sophisticated instruments. Without the effective functioning of these instruments, it would be impossible for him to chart the safest and most efficient course for the ship to follow.

One day the navigator realised that one of his most important instruments was incorrectly calibrated. As a result, he provided the captain inaccurate navigational information to use in making the decisions necessary to safely and efficiently direct the ship. No one but the navigator knew of this calibration problem, and the navigator decided not to inform the captain. He was afraid that the captain would blame him for not detecting the problem sooner and then require him to find a way to more accurately report the measurements. That would require a lot of work.

As a result, the navigator always made sure he slept near a lifeboat so that if the erroneous navigational information led to a disaster, he wouldn't go down with the ship. The ship eventually hit a reef that the captain believed to be miles away. The ship was lost, the cargo was lost and many sailors lost their lives. The navigator, always in close proximity to the lifeboats, survived the sinking and later became the navigator on another ship.

THE PERILS OF POOR MANAGERIAL ACCOUNTING

The story continues. Centuries later, there was a management accountant who worked for a company in which a great deal of money was invested. It was the job of this management accountant to provide information on how the company had performed, its current financial position, and the likely consequences of decisions being considered by the company's president and managers. In the performance of his duties, the management accountant relied on a managerial cost accounting system that was believed to represent the economics of the company. Without the effective functioning of the costing practices reported from this system, it would be impossible for the accountant to provide the president with the accurate and relevant cost information he needed to make economically sound decisions.

One day the management accountant realised that the calculations and practices on which the cost system was based were incorrect. It did not reflect the economic realities of the company. The input data was correct, but the reported information was flawed. As a result, the current and forward-looking information he provided to support the president's decision making was incorrect. No one but the management accountant knew this problem existed. He decided not to inform the president. He was afraid that the president would blame him for not detecting the problem sooner and require him to go through the agonising effort of developing and implementing a new, more accurate and relevant cost system. That would require a lot of work.

Meanwhile, the management accountant always made sure he kept his network with other professionals intact in case he had to find another position. Not surprisingly, the president's poorly informed pricing, investment and other decisions led the company into bankruptcy. The company went out of business, the owners lost their investment, creditors incurred financial losses and many hard-working employees lost their jobs. However, the management accountant easily found a job at another company.

THE ACCOUNTANT AS A BAD NAVIGATOR

What is the moral of the story? The *2003 Survey of Best Accounting Practices*, conducted by Ernst & Young and the Institute of Management Accountants, showed that 98% of the top financial executives surveyed believed that the cost information they supplied management to support their decisions was inaccurate. It further revealed that 80% of those financial executives did not plan on doing anything about it. I realise a decade has passed since the survey was conducted, but my unscientific observations, anecdotal evidence and heated online discussion group complaints makes me conclude that not much has changed.

The widely accepted solution is misallocated costing to apply activity-based cost management (ABC/M) principles not just to product and standard service line costs, but also to various types of distribution channels and types of customers. The goal is to apply direct costs to whatever consumes resources. For resources that are shared, these costs are to be traced using measurable drivers that reflect the consumption rate—not arbitrary and broad-brushed averages for cost allocations.

When one compares the properly calculated costs and profit margins using ABC/M principles to costing methods that violate the key accounting principle of cause and effect, the differences are surprisingly huge. The company makes and loses money in opposite areas from what the numbers show. This creates false beliefs throughout the organisation.

Why do so many accountants behave so irresponsibly? The list of answers is long. Some believe the error is not that big. Some think that extra administrative effort required to collect and calculate the new information will not offset the benefits of better decision making. Some think costs don't matter because the focus should be on sales growth. Whatever reasons are cited, accountants' resistance to change is based less on ignorance and more on misconceptions about accurate costing.

Doug Hicks observed to me, 'Today commercial ABC/M software and their associated analytics have dramatically reduced their efforts to report good managerial accounting information, and the benefits are widely heralded.' Furthermore, the preferred ABC/M implementation method is rapid prototyping with iteratively scaled modelling, which has destroyed myths about ABC/M being too complicated. By leveraging only a few key employees and a lot of estimates, usable ABC/M results as a repeatable reporting system are produced in weeks, not years. The main challenge in implementing ABC is designing and building the model, which is what the rapid prototyping method solves through doing—make your mistakes early and often.

Reasonably accurate cost and profit information is one of the pillars of performance management's portfolio of integrated methodologies. Accountants unwilling to adopt logical costing methods and managers who tolerate the perpetuation of flawed reporting should change their ways. Stay on the ship or get off the ship before real damage is done.

4

A TAXONOMY OF ACCOUNTING AND COSTING METHODS

Organisations possess a growing desire to understand their costs and the behaviour of what drives their costs. An organisation's managerial accounting system design can help or hinder its organisation's journey toward completing the full vision of enterprise performance management as I have defined it. It is understandable that people with nonfinancial backgrounds and training have difficulties understanding accounting. For many of them, accounting is outside their comfort zone.

However there is a gathering storm in the community of management accountants in which a need for so-called 'advanced' accounting techniques (eg, activity-based costing management, resource consumption accounting, lean accounting and time-driven activity-based costing) is confusing even the trained accountants, as well as the seasoned practitioners. The result is that managers and employees receive mixed messages about what costs are the correct costs. Upon closer inspection, various costing methods do not necessarily compete. They can co-exist and be reconciled and combined. They all do the same thing. They measure the consumption of economic resources.

CONFUSION ABOUT ACCOUNTING METHODS

The fields of law and medicine advance each decade because their body of knowledge is codified. Attorneys and physicians build upon their predecessor's captured learning over the centuries. In a sense, the generally accepted accounting principles (GAAP) published by the USA's Financial Accounting Standards Board (FASB) and the International Financial Reporting Standards (IFRS) organisations have also codified rules and principles. Financial accounting standards support external reporting for government regulatory agencies, bankers and the investment community.

Unfortunately, unlike financial accounting with its codification, managerial accounting has no such framework or set of universal standards. Accountants are left to their own devices, which typically are the methods and treatments at their organisation that they inherit from prior accountants who they succeeded. Accountants work long hours, with lots of daily problems to solve, so getting around to improving (or reforming) their organisation's management accounting practices and information to benefit their managers and employees is not a frequent occurrence. The escalation of compliance reporting, such as the USA's Sarbanes-Oxley Act of 2002 or India's Clause 49, is a major distraction from investing time to evaluate improvements to the organisation's managerial accounting system.

In the field of accounting, although rules are many, principles are few. Sadly, many accountants apparently are not aware that the purpose of managerial accounting is to provide data that generates questions and influences peoples' behaviour and supports good planning, control and decision making. Of course, how to apply cost information for decision support can lead to heated debates. For example, what is the incremental cost for delivering one additional customer order? To start, that answer depends on several assumptions, but if the debaters agree on them, then the robustness of the costing system and the resulting accuracy requirement to make the correct decision for that question might justify an advanced costing methodology.

Another accounting principle is 'precision is a myth.' There is no such thing as a correct cost because the cost of something is determined (ie, calculated) based on assumptions that an organisation has latitude to make. For example, should we include or exclude a sunk cost, such as equipment depreciation, in a product's cost? The answer depends on the type of decision being made. It is this latitude that is causing increasing confusion amongst accountants. If we step back, we can see that an organisation can refine its managerial accounting system over time through various stages of maturity. Changes to managerial accounting methods and treatments typically are not continuous, and they occur as infrequent and sizably punctuated reforms.

To assure we are oriented, let me be clear that the topic we are discussing in this book is managerial accounting. Under the big umbrella of accounting, there is also bookkeeping, financial accounting for external reporting and tax accounting. Those are peripheral to enterprise performance management. The purpose of management accounting information should be viewed as having two broad uses:

- *A cost autopsy (historical, descriptive)*. This information uses cost accounting information for analysis of what already happened in past time periods. My reference to costs as an 'autopsy' is quite morbid. However, the money was spent, and cost information reports where it went. Types of analysis include actual versus budgeted spending for cost variance analysis, activity cost analysis, product profitability, benchmarking and performance measure monitoring.

- *Decision support (future, predictive)*. This planning and control information serves as economic analysis to support decisions to drive improvement. It involves numerous assumptions, such as what-if volume and mix based on projections and draws on prior economic cost behaviour and rates for its calculations. Types of analysis include price and profit margin analysis, capital expenditures, outsourcing decisions, make-or-buy, project evaluation, incremental (or marginal) expense analysis, and rationalisation of products, channels and customers.

To be clear, the relatively higher value-add for performance improvement comes from decision support compared to cost autopsy reporting. The good news is the administrative effort of costing for decision support is relatively less because the source information is typically used as needed and for infrequent decisions, such as when setting catalogue or list prices, rather than for daily operations. However, some organisations must quote prices daily for custom orders to a wide variety of customers, so it is important that their cost modelling supports profit margin analysis—whether they are on an incremental or fully-absorbed cost basis.

A HISTORICAL EVOLUTION OF MANAGERIAL ACCOUNTING

If we travel back through time and re-visit the weeks in which an organisation's initial managerial accounting system was initially constructed, we first realise that it is a spin-off or variant of the ongoing financial accounting system already in place. The nature of the organisation's purpose and the economic conditions it faces govern the initial financial accounting system design. So, for example, if the organisation's output is non-recurring with relatively short product or service life cycles, like constructing a building or executing a consulting engagement, then project accounting is the more appropriate method—a very high form of direct costing. Similarly, if the organisation is a manufacturer of unique, one-time, engineer-to-order products, then they will likely begin with a job-order cost accounting scheme.

In contrast, if the products made or standard service lines delivered (eg, a bank loan) are recurring, consequently, the associated employee work activities will also be recurring. As a result, the initial financial accounting method may likely take on a standard costing approach (of which activity-based costing is simply a variant). In this case the repeating material requirements and time requirements for task labour are first measured. Then, the equivalent costs for both direct material and labour are assumed as a constant average and applied in total based on the quantity and volume of output (products made or services delivered). Of course, the actual expenses paid each accounting period to third parties and employees will always slightly differ from these averaged costs that were calculated 'at standard.' So there are various methods of cost variance analysis (eg, volume variance, labour rate or price variance, etc) to report what actually happened relative to what was planned and expected.

The overarching point here is that an organisation's initial condition—the types of products and services it makes and delivers as well as its expense structure—governs its initial managerial accounting methodology.

AN ACCOUNTING FRAMEWORK AND TAXONOMY

A need exists for an overarching framework to describe how expenses are measured as costs and to be used in decision making. An understandable framework is not difficult to construct and articulate. A framework I created for the International Federation of Accountants (www.ifac.org) is described here.

Figure 4-1 illustrates the large domain of accounting with three components: tax accounting, financial accounting and managerial accounting. The figure is similar to taxonomies that biologists use to understand plant and animal kingdoms. A *taxonomy* defines the components that make up of a body of knowledge. In the figure, two types of data sources are displayed at the upper right. The upper source is from financial transactions and bookkeeping, such as purchases and payroll. The lower source is non-financial measures, such as payroll hours worked, retail items sold or gallons of liquid produced.

Figure 4-1: Domain of Accounting

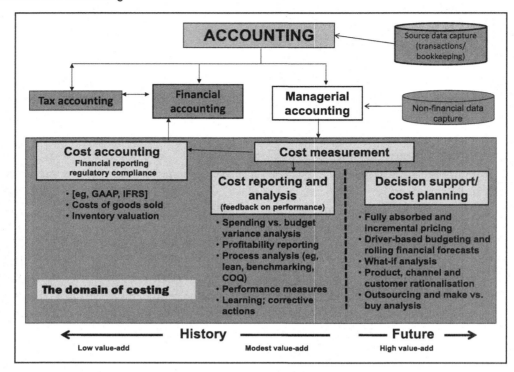

Source: Cokins, Gary. 'A Costing Levels Continuum Maturity Model.' International Federation of Accountants, 2012, www.ifac. org/publications-resources/evaluating-costing-journey-costing-levels-continuum-maturity-model.

As earlier mentioned, the financial accounting component is intended for external reporting, such as for regulatory agencies, banks, shareholders and the investment community. This information is compulsory. Financial accounting is governed by laws and rules established by regulatory agencies. In most nations, financial accounting follows GAAP. Some people jokingly refer to this as the 'GAAP trap' because focusing on these numbers may distract the organisation from more relevant accounting data or prevent it from finding more appropriate ways to calculate costs and profit margins. Financial accounting's purpose is for economic valuation. As such, it is typically not adequate or sufficient for internal decision making.

The tax accounting component in the figure has its own world of legislated rules.

Our area of concern is the management accounting component. It is used internally by managers and employee teams for insights and decision making. If you violate the financial accounting laws, you may go to jail. However you don't risk going to jail if you have poor managerial accounting, but your organisation runs the risk of making bad decisions. This is relevant because the margin of error is getting slimmer as the pressure grows for better organisational performance.

To oversimplify a distinction between financial and managerial accounting, financial accounting is about valuation, and managerial accounting is about value creation through good decision making.

The managerial accounting component in Figure 4-1 comprises three parts that are all recipients of inputs from the 'Cost Measurement' procedure of transforming incurred expenses (or their obligations) into calculated costs:

- *Cost accounting* represents the assignment of expenses into outputs, such as the cost of goods sold and the value of inventories. This box primarily provides external reporting to comply with regulatory agencies.

- *Cost reporting and analysis* represents the insights, inferences and analysis of what has already taken place in the business, that is, historical information, in order to understand and monitor performance.

- *Decision support with cost planning* involves decision making. It represents using the historical cost reporting information and its rates in combination with other economic information, including forecasts and planned changes (eg, processes, products, services, channels) in order to test, validate and make the types of decisions that lead to a financially successful and sustained future.

It will be apparent that the key differentiator between cost accounting and the other two uses of cost measurement is that cost accounting is deeply constrained by regulatory practices and describing the past in accordance with rules of financial accounting. The other two categories offer diagnostic support to interpret and draw inferences from what has already taken place and for what can happen in the future. Cost reporting and analysis is about explanation. Decision support with cost planning is about possibilities and probabilities.

Asking What? So What? Then What?

An important message at the bottom of Figure 4-1 is that the value, utility and usefulness of the information increases, arguably at an exponential rate, moving from the left side to the right side of the diagram.

In Figure 4-1 the cost accounting data establishes a foundation; it is of low value for decision making. The cost reporting for analysis information converts cost measurement data into a context. It is useful for managers and employee teams to clearly observe outcomes with transparency that may have never been seen before or is dramatically different from their existing beliefs derived from their firm's less mature cost measurement method. Cost reporting displays the reality of what has happened and provides answers to the 'What?' question. That is, for example, what did things cost last period?

However, an obvious follow-up question should be 'So what?' That is, based on any questionable or bothersome observations, is there merit to making changes and interventions? How relevant to improving performance is the outcome we are seeing? This leads to the more critical and relatively higher value-added need to propose actions—to make and take decisions—surfaced from cost planning. This is the 'Then what?' question. For example, what change can be made or action taken (such as a distributor altering its truck and rail distribution routes), and what is the ultimate impact? Of course, changes will lead to multiple effects on service levels, quality and delivery times, but the economic effect on profits and costs should also be considered. This gets to the heart of the widening gap between accountants and decision makers that use accounting data. To close the gap, accountants must change their mindset from managerial accounting to managerial economics, sometimes referred to as *decision-based costing*.

There is a catch. When the 'Cost Reporting and Analysis' component shifts right toward the 'Decision Support With Cost Planning' box in Figure 4-1, then analysis shifts to the realm of decision support via economic analysis. For example, one needs to understand the impact that changes will have on future expenses. Therefore, the focus now shifts to resources and their capacities, which require expenses. This involves classifying the behaviour of resource expenses as sunk, fixed, semi-fixed or variable with changes in service offerings, volumes, mix, processes and the like. This can be tricky. A key concept for these classifications is that the 'adjustability of capacity' of any individual resource expense depends on both the planning time horizon and the ease or difficulty of adjusting the individual resource's capacity (ie, its stickability). This wanders into the messy area of marginal expense analysis that textbooks oversimplify but is complicated to accurately calculate in the real world.

Predictive Versus Descriptive Accounting

Figure 4-2 illustrates how a firm's view of its profit and expense structure changes as analysis shifts from the historical cost reporting view to a predictive cost planning view. The latter is the context from which decisions are considered and evaluated.

Figure 4-2: Descriptive Versus Predictive Accounting

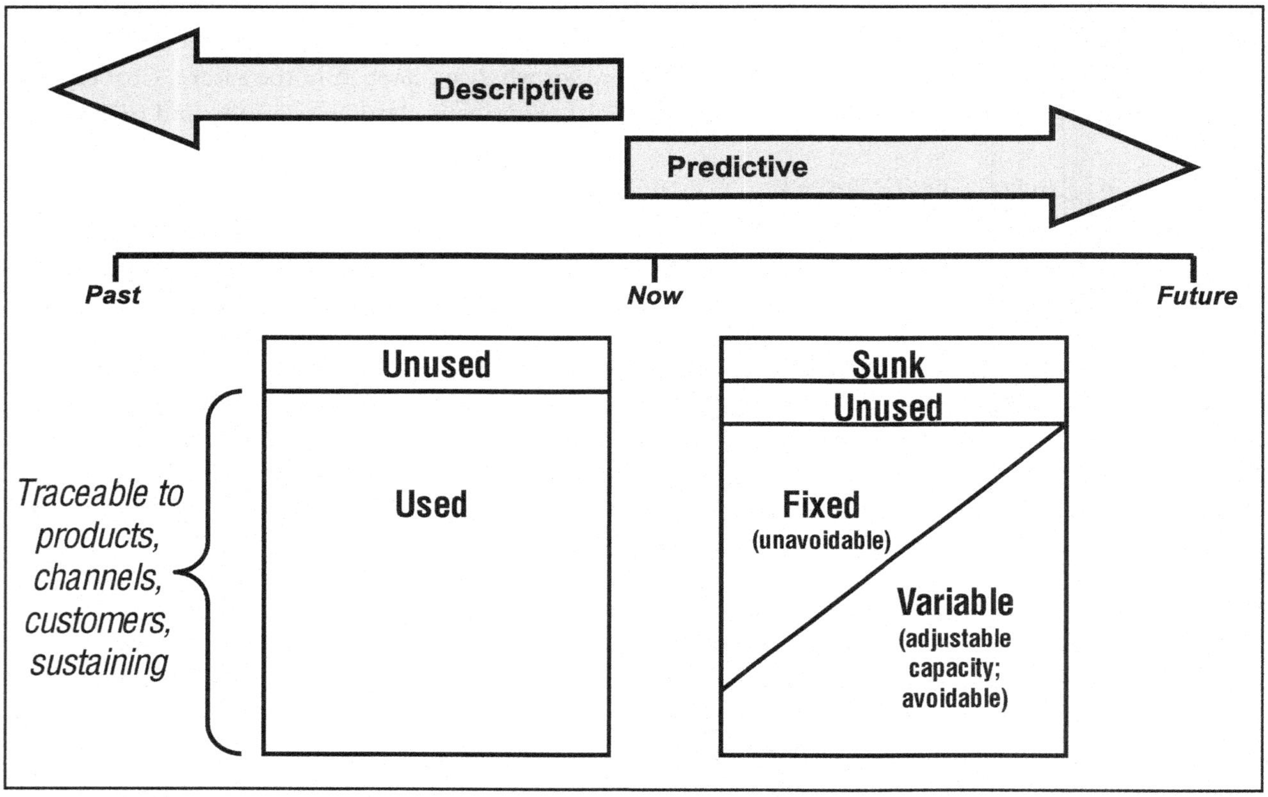

Source: Copyright Gary Cokins. Used with permission.

On the left-hand side of the figure, during the historical time period, the expenses were incurred. The capacity these expenses were incurred for were supplied, and then they were either (1) unused as idle or protective capacity, or (2) used to make products, deliver customer services or to internally sustain the organisation. This is the cost reporting and analysis component from Figure 4-1 that calculates output costs. The money was spent, and costing answers where it was used. This is the descriptive view of costs. Accountants refer to this as *full absorption costing*, when all the expenses for a past time period are totally traced to outputs. It traces expenses (and hopefully does not allocate expenses on causal insensitive broad averages) to measure which outputs (eg, products) uniquely consumed the resources. Full absorption costing uses direct costing methods, which are relatively easy to apply, and ideally supplements the reporting with activity-based costing techniques for the indirect and shared expenses, which are trickier to model, calculate and report.

In contrast, Figure 4-2's right-hand side is the predictive view of costs—the decision support with cost planning component from Figure 4-1. In the future, the capacity levels and types of resources can be adjusted. Capacity only exists as a resource, not as a process or work activity. The classification of an expense as sunk, fixed, semi-fixed or variable depends on the planning time horizon. The diagonal line reveals that in the very short term, most expenses are not easily changed; hence, they are classified as fixed. As the time horizon extends into the future, capacity becomes adjustable. For example, assets can be leased, not purchased. Future workers can be contracted from a temporary employment agency, not hired as full-time employees. Therefore, these expenses are classified as variable.

In the predictive view of Figure 4-2, changes in demand, such as the forecasted volume and mix of products and services ordered from customers, will drive the consumption of processes (and the work activities that belong to them). In turn, this will determine what level of both fixed and variable resource expenses are needed to supply capacity for future use. For purchased assets, such as retail store display shelves or expensive equipment, these costs are classified as sunk costs. Their full capacity and associated expense were acquired when an executive authorised and signed his or her name to the purchase order for the vendor or contractor. Some idle capacity (such as staffing a customer call centre) is typically planned for. This deliberately planned idle capacity is intended to meet temporary demand surges or as an insurance buffer for the uncertainty of the demand forecast accuracy. Its cost is justified by offsetting potential lost revenues from unacceptable, low service levels to customers.

Because decisions only affect the future, the predictive view is the basis for analysis and evaluation. The predictive view applies techniques such as what-if analysis and simulations. These projections are based on forecasts and consumption rates. However, consumption rates are ideally derived as calibrated rates from the historical, descriptive view, when the rate of operational work typically remains constant until productivity and process improvements affect them. These rates are for both direct expenses and rates that can be calibrated from an activity-based costing model for the indirect and shared expenses. When improvements or process changes occur, the calibrated historical consumption rates can be adjusted up or down from the valid baseline measure that is already being experienced. Accountants refer to these projections as *marginal expense analysis*. For example, as future incremental demands change from the existing, near-term baseline operations, how is the supply for needed capacity affected?

This topic of marginal expense analysis will be later covered in Part 4 on planning, budgeting and forecasting.

CO-EXISTING COST ACCOUNTING METHODS

Confusion can arise because some costing methods calculate and report different costs that are not just variations in cost accuracy but are also different reported costs altogether. This raises the question, 'Should there be two or more different, co-existing cost reporting methods that report dissimilar numbers?' For example, one tactical costing method is used for operations (eg, lean accounting) and making short-term decisions. Another strategic costing method (for planning, marketing, pricing and sales analysts to evaluate profit margins) is used for longer-term decisions.

There will be debates, but, eventually, some form of consensus will triumph within an organisation. The underlying arguments may be due to the inappropriate usage of standard costing information—and potential inappropriate decisions and actions that may result. However there may be a deeper problem. Cost accounting system data is not the same thing as cost information that should be used for decision making. As described in Figure 4-2, the majority of value from cost information for decision making is not in historical reports— the descriptive view. Its primary value comes from planning the future (such as product and customer rationalisation), marginal expense analysis for one-off decisions or trade-off analysis between two or more alternatives.

The good news is that organisations are challenging traditional managerial accounting practices. So in the end, any accounting treatments that yield better decision making should prevail. The co-existence of two or more costing approaches may cause confusion over which one reports the correct cost. But that is a different problem. What matters is that organisations are seeking better ways to apply managerial accounting techniques to make better decisions.

5

MANAGERIAL ACCOUNTING DESIGN COMPLYING WITH THE CAUSALITY PRINCIPLE

Up to this point in the book, concepts and principles have been covered, including references to activity-based cost management (ABC/M) principles. In this chapter, the design of a managerial accounting system is discussed. Because ABC/M principles are essential, this chapter begins with it as a topic.

REMOVING THE BLINDFOLD WITH ABC/M

Imagine that you and three friends go to a restaurant. You order a small salad, and they each order an expensive prime rib and a glass of wine. When the waiter brings the bill, your three friends say, 'Let's split the bill evenly.' How would you feel?

This is how many products and service lines also feel when the accountants take a large amount of indirect and support overhead expenses and allocate them as costs without any logic. There is minimal or no causal link that reflects a true relative consumption of the expenses by the individual products, service lines or end-users. This is unfair. ABC/M more fairly 'splits the bill' based on what was individually ordered. Many ABC/M practitioners wish the word *allocation* never existed. It implies inequity to managers and employees based on past abuses in their organisation's accounting practices. The word *allocation* effectively means 'misallocation' because that is usually the result. ABC/M practitioners will often say that they do not allocate expenses. Instead they trace and assign them to costs based on cause and effect relationships.

ABC/M can do much more than simply trace expenses and costs. It provides a tremendous amount of visibility and transparency of costs for people to draw insights from and also use for predicting and validating the possible outcomes of decisions. Many operations people cynically believe that accountants count what is easily counted, but not what counts. Outdated, traditional accounting—broadly averaged cost allocations—blocks managers and employees from seeing the more relevant costs.

As a caution, it is a mistake for ABC/M project teams to refer to ABC/M as an improvement, project, programme or change initiative. ABC/M merely creates information. The ABC/M information is simply used as a means to an end. If ABC/M is described as an improvement programme, it might be regarded by managers and employees as a fad, fashion or 'project of the month.' ABC/M information makes visible the economics of the organisation and its consumption of resource expenses. Money is continuously being spent on organisational resources regardless of whether ABC/M measuring is present.

ABC/M is not just about supporting other initiatives but about driving some of those initiatives. An organisation is continuously using up its resources through its work activities and into its outputs regardless of whether ABC/M is monitoring these events. ABC/M is simply like a mirror, displaying expenses transformed into costs. When one realises that ABC/M is fundamentally good information to be used for understanding, discovery and decision making, then it is better positioned for longer-term use and wider acceptance. ABC/M's information can be a great enabler for providing answers. The key word here is *enabler*. One controller I met referred to ABC/M as the ultimate question generator. He observed that, equipped with the ABC/M information, employees and managers frequently had reactions like, 'What would explain or account for that?'

OVERHEAD EXPENSES ARE DISPLACING DIRECT EXPENSES

So why has ABC/M become popular? A primary reason has been a significant shift in most organisations' expense structures. What do I mean by a shift? The direct labourers in organisations are the employees who perform the frontline, repeating work that is closest to the products and customers. However, numerous other employees behind the frontline also do recurring support work on a daily or weekly basis. The support work done by these employees is highly repeatable at some level. Figure 5-1 is a chart that includes this type of indirect expense plus the other two major expense components of any organisation's cost structure, its purchased materials and its direct expenses.

Figure 5-1: Overhead Expenses Are Displacing Direct Expenses

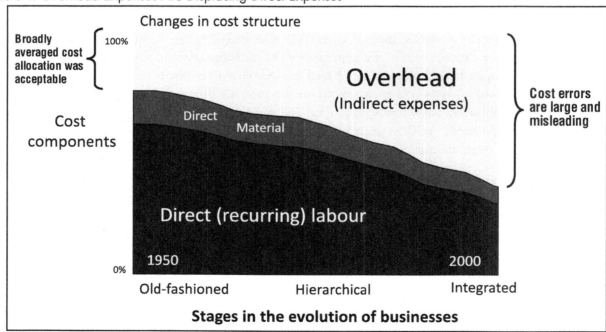

Source: Copyright Gary Cokins. Used with permission.

Most organisations are experienced at monitoring and measuring the work of the labourers who do recurring work (direct expenses). For these expenses, cost rates and standard costs are reported. The bottom layer of the figure contains cost information that also reveals performance-related costs other than the period's spending, such as labour cost variance reporting. It is in this area of the figure, for example, that manufacturers use labour routings and process sheets to measure efficiency. These costs are well known by the name *standard costs*. Service organisations also measure this type of output-related information. For example, many banks know their standard cost for each type of deposit, each type of wire transfer and so forth.

Problems occur in the indirect expense area appearing at the top portion of Figure 5-1. The figure reveals that over the last few decades, the support overhead[1] expenses have been displacing the recurring direct costs. The organisation already has substantial visibility of its recurring costs, but it does not have much insight for understanding its overhead or what is causing the level of spending of its overhead. ABC/M helps provide visibility for insights and learning.

In a bank, for example, managers and employee teams do not get the same strong financial information about the vice presidents and other higher-ups as they do about bank clerks performing the recurring work. The only financial information available to analyse the expenses of the vice presidents and other support overhead is the annual financial budget data. These levels of expenses are annually negotiated. The focus is on spending levels, not on the various cost rates to perform work. The expense spending is monitored after the budget is published. Spending is only monitored for each department or function for each period to see if the managers' spending performance is under or over their budget or plan.

ABC/M merely extends to the indirect and shared expenses the same type of understanding and visibility of spending that is already applied to the recurring direct workers. It is not complicated. Basically ABC/M becomes an organisation-wide method of understanding work activity costs as well as the standard costs of outputs.

IMPACT OF DIVERSITY IN PRODUCTS, SERVICE LINES, CHANNELS AND CUSTOMERS

When you ask people why they believe indirect and overhead expenses are displacing direct expenses, most answer that it is because of technology, equipment, automation or computers. In other words, organisations are automating what previously were manual jobs. However this is only a secondary factor for explaining the shift in organisational expense components.

The primary cause for the shift is the gradual proliferation in types of products and service lines. Over the last few decades organisations have been increasingly offering a greater variety of products and services, as well as using more types of distribution and sales channels. For example, with products more colours, sizes and ranges have been offered. In addition, organisations have been servicing more and different types of customers. Introducing greater variation and diversity (ie, heterogeneity) into an organisation creates complexity, and this increasing complexity results in more indirect expenses to manage it. So the fact that the overhead component of expense is displacing the recurring direct labour expense does not automatically mean that an organisation is becoming inefficient or bureaucratic. It simply means that the company is offering more variety to different types of customers.

In summary, the shift of indirect expenses displacing direct labour reveals the cost of complexity, which is mainly customer-driven. ABC/M does not fix or simplify complexity. The complexity is a result of other things. However what ABC/M does do is point out where the complexity is and where it comes from.

How long can organisations go on making decisions with the misinformation reported by their accounting systems? In the 1980s many organisations, reacting to the pressures from high-quality Japanese products, confessed that they had a 'quality crisis.' In the 21st century, organisations may realise that they have a 'management accounting crisis.'

GROWING DISCONTENT WITH TRADITIONAL CALCULATION OF COSTS

Why do managers shake their heads in disbelief when they think about their company's cost accounting system? I once heard an operations manager complain, 'You know what we think of our cost accounting system? It is a bunch of fictitious lies—but we all agree to them.' It is a sad thing to see the users of the accounting data resign themselves to lack of hope. Unfortunately, some accountants are comfortable when the numbers all foot and tie and could care less if the parts making up the total are incorrect. The total is all that matters to them, and any arbitrary cost allocation can tie out to the total. It is just math.

The sad truth is that when employees and managers are provided with reports that have flawed and misleading accounting data in them, they have little choice but to use that information regardless of its validity or their scepticism of its integrity. Mind you, they are using the data to draw conclusions and make decisions, which is risky.

How can traditional accounting, which has been around for so many years, suddenly be considered so bad? The answer is that the existing data are not necessarily bad as it is quite distorted, incomplete and unprocessed. Figure 5-2 shows the first hint of the problem. The left side shows the classic monthly responsibility-centre expense statement report that managers receive. Note that the example used is the back office of an insurance company. It is quite like a factory, which demonstrates that, despite misconceptions, indirect white collar workers produce outputs no differently than do factory workers.

If you ask managers who routinely receive this report questions such as, 'How much of these expenses can you control or influence? How much insight do you get into the content of work of your employees?' they will likely answer both questions with, 'Not much!' This is because the salary and fringe benefit expenses usually make up the most sizeable portion of controllable expenses, and all that the manager sees are those expenses reported as lump-sum amounts. In short, they see what was spent but not what caused varying levels of spending or to what (ie, products) or whom (ie, customers) it is traced.

Figure 5-2: The Language of ABC/M

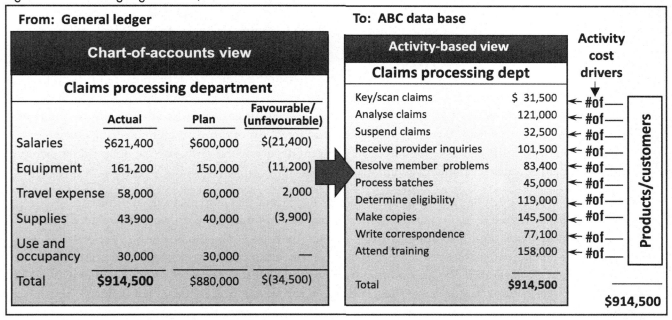

Source: Copyright Gary Cokins. Used with permission.

When you translate those 'Chart of Account' expenses into the work activities that consume the financial general ledger's expenses, a manager's insights from viewing the activity costs begin to increase. The right side of Figure 5-2 is the ABC/M view of the left side that is used for analysis and as the starting point for calculating the costs for both processes (and the work activities that belong to them) and their diverse outputs. In effect, the ABC/M view resolves the deficiencies of traditional financial accounting by focusing on work activities. ABC/M is work-centric, whereas the general ledger is transaction-centric. To be clear, the left side general ledger cost centre report is not bad, but the format of the data is structurally deficient to trace and assign those expenses into process and output costs. ABC/M reformats that data.

Here is a critical concept. Expenses are not the same thing as costs. What are the differences? *Expenses* are defined as an organisation exchanging money with third parties, such as paying suppliers or paying its employees' salaries. (Expenses may also be near-cash balance sheet liabilities that reflect the obligation to pay cash in the near future.) In short, currency exits the treasury. In contrast, costs are always calculated costs. Costs reflect the use of the spending of the expenses. That is, from the expenses, all costs follow. Costs are calculated representations of how those expenses flow through work activities and into the outputs of work, that is, products, services, channels and customers.

ACTIVITIES ARE EXPRESSED WITH ACTION VERBS

A key difference between ABC/M and the general ledger and traditional techniques of cost allocation (ie, absorption costing) is that ABC/M describes activities using an 'action verb-adjective-noun' grammar convention, such as 'inspect defective products,' 'open new customer accounts,' or 'process customer claims.' This gives ABC/M its flexibility. Such wording is powerful because managers and employee teams can better relate to these phrases, and the wording implies that the work activities can be favourably affected, changed, improved or eliminated. The general ledger uses a chart of accounts, whereas ABC/M uses a chart of activities. In translating general ledger data to work activities and processes, ABC/M preserves the total reported turnovers and costs but allows the turnovers, budgeted funding and costs to be viewed differently— and better.

Notice how inadequate the data in the 'Chart of Accounts' view in the figure are for reporting business process costs that run cross-functionally, penetrating the vertical and artificial, silo-like boundaries of the organisation chart. The general ledger is organised around separate departments or cost centres. This presents a reporting problem. For example, with a manufacturer, what is the true total cost of processing engineering change notices (ECNs) that travel through so many hands in different departments? For a service organisation, what is the true cost of opening a new customer account?

Many organisations have been flattened and de-layered to the extent that employees from different departments or cost centres frequently perform similar activities and multi-task in two or more core business processes. Only by re-assembling and aligning the work activity costs across the business processes, such as 'process ECNs' or 'open new customer accounts,' can the end-to-end process costs be seen, measured and eventually managed. As a result of the general ledger's structure of cost centre mapping to the hierarchical organisation chart, its information drives vertical behaviour, it does not process behaviour, which is much more functional and desirable.

Managing with a process view has created a growing need for better managerial and costing data. Managing processes and managing activities (ie, costs) go together. By defining a *business process* as comprising two or more logically related work activities intended to serve end customers, the need for integrating processes, outputs and measured costs becomes even more apparent as an important requirement for managers and teams. There are two ways to organise and analyse ABC/M work activity cost data: (1) the *horizontal* process view sequences and additively builds-up costs, whereas (2) the *vertical* cost assignment view transforms resource expenses into output costs by continuously re-assigning costs based on causal-based tracing (ie, cost allocations). I will further describe both views in a few pages. The primary focus in this book is this latter vertical view, popularly called *absorption accounting.* Activity-based costing is more associated with this latter view.

By using traditional cost systems, managers are usually denied visibility of many of the costs that belong to the end-to-end business processes. This is particularly apparent in the stocking, distribution, marketing and selling costs that traditional accounting 'expenses to the month's period.' With traditional cost allocations, these sales, general, and administrative expenses are not proportionately traced to the costs of the unique products, containers, services, channels or customers that cause those costs to occur.

I am often asked to explain Figure 5-2 in the simplest terms. I humorously reply, 'The right side is good because the left side is bad!' Now I did not say the general ledger is a bad thing. In fact, it is just the opposite. The general ledger is a wonderful instrument for what it was designed to do—accumulate spending transactions into their accounts. Repeating my earlier point, the data in that format is structurally deficient for decision support other than the most primitive form of control, budget variances. Translating it into calculated costs corrects this deficiency.

DRIVERS TRIGGER THE WORKLOAD COSTS

Much more information can be gleaned from the right side view of Figure 5-2. Look at the second activity, 'Analyse claims' for $121,000, and ask what would make that activity cost significantly increase or decrease? The answer is the number of claims analysed, that is, that work's activity driver. Figure 5-2 shows that each activity, on a stand-alone basis, has its own activity driver. At this stage, the costing is no longer recognising the organisational chart and its artificial boundaries. The focus is now on the work that the organisation performs and what affects the level of that workload.

Additionally, let's assume there were 1,000 claims analysed during that period for the department shown in Figure 5-2. The unit cost per each analysed claim is $100 per claim. If a specific group of old-age pensioners over the age of 65 were responsible for half of those claims, we would know more about a specific customer or beneficiary of that work. The old-age pensioners would have caused $60,500 of that work (ie, 500 claims multiplied by $121 per claim). If married couples with small children required another fraction, married couples with grown children a different fraction, and so forth, ABC/M would trace all of the $121,000. If each of the other work activities were similarly traced using the unique activity driver for each activity, ABC/M would pile up the entire $914,500 into each group of beneficiary. This re-assignment of the resource expenses would be much more accurate than any general cost allocation applied in traditional costing procedures and their broad averages. ABC/M complies with cost accounting's causality principle—a cause and effect relationship. Arbitrary cost allocations do not.

This cost assignment network is one of the major reasons that ABC/M calculates more accurate costs of outputs. As earlier mentioned, the terms *tracing* or *assigning* are preferable to the term *cost allocation* because many people associate the *allocation* with a re-distribution of costs that have little to no correlation between source and destinations. Hence, to some organisations, overhead cost allocations are rejected by users as arbitrary and are cynically viewed.

When managers receive the left side responsibility expense centre report in Figure 5-2, they are either happy or sad, but rarely any smarter. In summary, the general ledger view describes what was spent, whereas the activity-based view describes what it was spent for and what caused the cost. The ledger records the expenses, and the activity view calculates the costs of work activities, processes and all outputs, such as products. Intermediate output costs, such as the unit cost to process a transaction, are also calculated in the activity view. When employees have reliable and relevant information, managers can manage less and lead more.

The assignment of the resource expenses demonstrates that all costs actually originate with the customer or beneficiary of the work, not with the general ledger. This is the opposite of what accountants who perform cost allocations think about costs. Cost allocations are structured as a one source-to-many destinations redistribution of cost. However the destinations actually are the origin for the expenses. In Figure 5-2, the destinations, usually outputs or people, place demands on work, and the work activities draw on the resources and capacity. Then, in the opposite direction, the costs measure the effect by reflecting backward through an ABC/M cost assignment network. Costing is modelling, not bookkeeping.

This may sound ironic, but cost management can be considered an oxymoron (like controlled chaos). You do not really manage costs and financial results. That is like pushing a rope. You understand the causes (and drivers) of costs. Then you manage the causes. Cost management is accomplished by driver management. So, in effect, an organisation does not manage its costs. It manages what causes those costs to occur (ie, its cost drivers) and the effectiveness and efficiency of the organisations' people and equipment to respond to those causal triggers.

Today's competitive world will be dominated by learning organisations, not ones that are limited by spending restrictions, such as from a budget. The right side of Figure 5-2 re-states those same expenses in a much more useful format and structure for decision support. Cost accounting is outside many individuals' comfort zones. ABC/M makes cost information understandable and logical. However when you have the wrong information coupled with the wrong measurements, it is not difficult to make wrong decisions.

STRATEGIC VERSUS OPERATIONAL ABC/M

A common misconception is that organisations use only a single, enterprise-wide ABC/M system. There can actually be multiple ABC/M systems constructed for a single organisation. There are two broad users and decision makers of ABC/M data: strategic versus operational. In fact, two types of ABC/M model designs serve each type of user, but they both follow the same cost assignment mechanics based on the causality principle. The difference between them is the scope of expenses included plus the inclusion or exclusion of pricing or turnover data for calculating profit margins.

Strategic ABC/M, also referred to here as *enterprise-wide ABC/M*, is about first doing the right things, that is, selling profitable products and services to customers that are also profitable. Strategic ABC/M is about enhancing turnovers and assuring higher profits based on the product's or service's value to draw good prices and the considering varying levels of demanding behaviour of different types of customers.

Operational ABC/M, also referred to here as *local ABC/M*, is not enterprise-wide but, rather, addresses individual functions, departments or business processes. Its intent is not about analysing profit contribution margins but, rather, focuses on improving process, more efficiently managing activity costs, taking out waste and optimising asset utilisation.

In short, the difference in ABC/M model design is as follows:

- *Strategic ABC/M* includes all of the enterprise expenses and then subtracts the traceable costs (to products, channels and customers) from sold line items (ie, pricing and turnovers) to compute the profit contribution margins.

- *Operational ABC/M* confines the expenses included to those mainly involved in the function, department or process. It focuses on analysing the work to remove waste, manage unused capacity, improve productivity and improve asset utilisation.

One of the values of commercial ABC/M software is that it can consolidate multiple *operational* ABC/M models into the parent, enterprise-wide *strategic* ABC/M model.

Endnotes

1 Organisations often refer to this support-related work as *overhead*. Overhead is also referred to as *indirect* and *shared expenses*. The term *overhead* can be misleading and often has a negative connotation. In many cases, overhead is a crucial and is a very positive thing to have. I will use *indirect* and *overhead* interchangeably or together to refer to this type of expense and cost. Regardless of which term is used, the objective of calculating costs is to properly trace them, not arbitrarily allocate them, to what is causing them—and in the proper proportions.

6

STRATEGIC COST MANAGEMENT FOR PRODUCT PROFITABILITY ANALYSIS

As previously described, some accountants preserve the status quo by defending their simplistic and arbitrary, broadly-averaged cost allocations of expenses without causal relationships as being adequate for product and service line costing and profit analysis. This practice may have been adequate in the past. The use of volume-based cost allocations will provide reasonably accurate, calculated costs only when the following conditions exist:

- Few and very similar products and service lines
- Low amount of indirect and shared expenses
- Homogeneous conversion processes
- Homogeneous channels, customer demands and customers
- Low selling, distribution, customer service and administrative expenses
- Very high profit margins

How many organisations possess those characteristics? Hardly any exist today. Perhaps simple cost allocations worked when Henry Ford was producing thousands of Model-T automobiles, all black, and with minimal indirect overhead expenses, but not anymore. The design and architecture of the activity-based cost management (ABC/M) cost assignment network provides the solution to calculate relatively more accurate costs and profit margins.

ABC/M IS A MULTI-LEVEL COST RE-ASSIGNMENT NETWORK

In complex, support-intensive organisations there can be a substantial chain of indirect and shared activities supporting the direct work activities that eventually trace into the final cost objects. These chains result in activity-to-activity assignments, and they rely on intermediate activity drivers in the same way that final cost objects rely on activity drivers to re-assign activity costs into them based on their diversity and variation.

The direct costing of indirect costs is no longer an insurmountable problem as it was in the past given the existence of commercial ABC/M software. ABC/M allows intermediate direct costing to a local process or to an internal customer or cost object that is causing the demand for work. That is, ABC/M cost flow assignment networks no longer have to stop work due to limited spreadsheet software that is restricted by columns-to-rows math. In contrast, ABC/M software is arterial in its design and allows costs to flow flexibly. Using this expense assignment and tracing network, ABC/M eventually re-assigns 100% of the enterprise's expenses into final product, service line, channel, customer and business sustaining costs. In short, ABC/M connects customers to the unique resources they consume—and in proportion to their consumption—as if ABC/M is an optical fibre network. Visibility to costs is provided everywhere throughout the cost assignment network, from a customer to all the resource expenses it is consuming.

With ABC/M, the demands on work are communicated via activity drivers and their driver cost rates. Activity driver cost rates can be thought of as very local burden rates. They re-assign expenses into costs with a more local, granular level than with traditional methods and with arterial flow streams, not with the accountant's rigid, step-down cost allocation method that reduces costing accuracy and is restricted to a single activity driver.

Examine the ABC/M cost assignment network in Figure 6-1, which consists of three modules connected by cost assignment paths. Imagine the cost assignment paths as pipes and straws in which the diameter of each path reflects the amount of cost flowing. The power of an ABC/M model is that the cost assignment paths and their destinations (ie, cost objects) provide traceability to assign costs from beginning to end, from resource expenses to costs for each type of (or each specific) customer—the origin for all costs and expenses.

Figure 6-1: ABC/M Cost Assignment Network

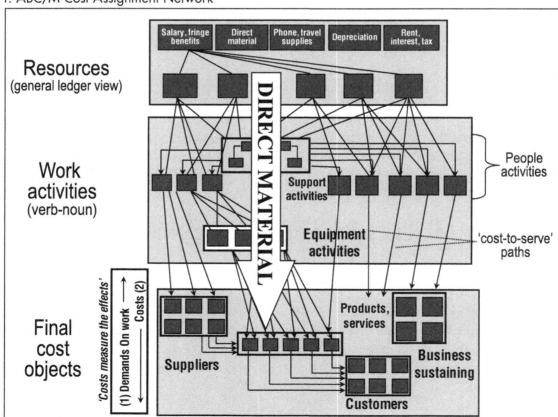

Source: Copyright Gary Cokins. Used with permission.

It may be useful to mentally reverse all the arrowheads in Figure 6-1. This polar switch reveals that all expenses originate with a demand-pull from customers, and the calculated costs simply measure the causal effect. The ABC/M network is basically a snapshot view of the organisation conducted during a specific time period.

Resources, at the top of the cost assignment network in Figure 6-1, are the capacity to perform work because they represent all the available means that work activities can draw on. Resources can be thought of as the organisation's chequebook because this is where all the period's expenditure transactions are accumulated and sorted into buckets of spending. Examples of resources are salaries, operating supplies or electrical power. These are the period's cash outlays and amortised cash outlays, such as for depreciation, from a prior period. It is during this step that the applicable resource drivers are developed as the mechanism to convert resource expenses into activity costs. A popular basis for tracing or assigning resource expenses is the time (eg, number of minutes) that people or equipment are performing activities. An alternative and popular resource driver is the percentage splits of time amongst activities, which is easier and accomplishes a comparable result. Although these proportions are estimated, the estimates are sufficient for adequate cost accuracy of final cost objects.

The activity module is where work is performed by people, equipment and assets. It is where resources are converted into some type of output. The activity cost assignment step contains the structure to assign activity costs to cost objects (or to other activities), utilising activity drivers as the mechanism to accomplish this assignment.

Cost objects, at the bottom of the cost assignment network, represent the broad variety of outputs, services and channels where costs accumulate. The customers are the final-final cost objects. Their existence ultimately creates the need for a cost structure in the first place. Cost objects are the persons or things that benefit from incurring work activities. Examples of cost objects are products, service lines, distribution channels, customers and outputs of internal processes. Cost objects can be thought of as the 'what' or 'for whom' that work activities are done.

Some activities in an organisation do not directly contribute to customer value, responsiveness and quality. That does not mean those activities can be eliminated or even reduced without doing harm to the business entity. For example, preparing required regulatory reports does not add to the value of any cost object or to the satisfaction of the customer. However, that type of work activity does have value to the organisation because it enables it to function in a legal manner. These types of activity costs are usually traced to a sustaining cost object group popularly called *business* (or *organisational*) *sustaining costs*. This modelling technique separates the business sustaining costs as not being involved with making or delivering a product or serving a customer. It prevents unfairly over-costing products or customers yet allows for all expenses to be traced (and, if needed, reconciled back to the general ledger or source systems (eg, payroll, purchasing). Business sustaining costs are described later in this chapter.

Although some people are initially intimidated by Figure 6-1, it makes more sense the more you work with ABC/M. Also, the ABC/M cost assignment network is related to an observation that has become known as Metcalf's Law, which states 'The value of a network increases as the number of nodes increases.'

My conclusion about ABC/M is that the key to a good ABC/M system is the design and architecture of its cost assignment network. It is also the primary determinant of accuracy of final cost objects. (The topic of cost accuracy is later discussed.) The nodes are the sources and destinations through which all the expenses are re-assigned into costs. Their configuration helps deliver the utility and value of the data for decision making.

DRIVERS: RESOURCE, COST, ACTIVITY AND COST OBJECT DRIVERS

There is probably no term, other than *activity*, that has become more identified with ABC/M than the term *driver* and its several variations. The problem is a driver is used in several ways with varying meanings. To be very clear, a *cost driver* is something that can be described in words but not necessarily in numbers. For example, a storm would be a cost driver that results in much clean-up work activities and their resulting costs. In contrast, the *activity drivers* in ABC/M's cost assignments must be quantitative. They use measures, including percentage splits, that apportion costs to cost objects. In the ABC/M vertical cost assignment view, there are three types of drivers, and all are required to be quantitative:

- Resource drivers trace expenditures (cash outlays, such as salaries) to work activities.
- Activity drivers trace activity costs to cost objects.
- Cost object drivers trace cost object costs to other cost objects.

In the ABC/M vertical cost assignment view, activity drivers will have their own higher order cost drivers, as in the storm example. Cost drivers and activity drivers serve different purposes. Activity drivers are output measures that reflect the usage of each work activity, and they must be quantitatively measurable. An activity driver, which relates a work activity to cost objects, meters out the work activity based on the unique diversity and variation of the cost objects that are consuming the work activity. A cost driver is a driver of a higher order than activity drivers. A storm was the previously mentioned example. One cost driver can affect multiple activities. A cost driver need not be measurable but can simply be described as a triggering event. The term describes the larger scale causal event that influences the frequency, intensity or magnitude of a workload and, therefore, it influences the amount of work done that translates to the cost of the activities.

The third type of driver—a *cost object driver*—applies to cost objects after all activity costs have already been logically assigned. Note that cost objects can be consumed or used by other cost objects. For example, when a specific customer purchases a mix of products, similar to you placing different items in your grocery cart than another shopper, the quantities purchased are a cost object driver. The source data is typically from the sales or invoicing system.

BUSINESS AND ORGANISATIONAL SUSTAINING COSTS

As previously mentioned, certain types of activity costs trace to business sustaining cost objects, which is similar to other types that trace to product, service line and customer cost objects. The structure of expanded ABC/M systems capitalises on the use of sustaining activities traced to sustaining cost objects to segregate product and customer-related activity costs or to segment product or customer activity costs that cannot be identified as specific to unique products or customers.

Business or infrastructure sustaining costs are those costs not caused by products or customer service needs. The consumption of these costs cannot be logically or causally traced to products, services, customers or service recipients. One example is the closing of the books each month by the accounting department. How can one measure which product caused more or less of that work? One cannot.

Another example is a green lawn. Which customers or products cause the grass to grow? These kinds of activity cost cannot be directly charged to a customer, product or service in any fair and equitable way. There is simply no 'use-based' causality originating from the product or customer. (Yet, overhead expenses are routinely and unfairly allocated this way despite the result being flawed and misleading costs.) Recovering these costs through pricing or funding may eventually be required, but that is a different issue. The issue here is fairly charging cost objects when no causal relationship exists and preventing overstating their costs.

Business-sustaining costs (or organisation-sustaining costs for governments and not-for-profit organisations) can eventually be fully absorbed into products or customers, but such a cost allocation is blatantly arbitrary. There simply is no cause and effect relationship between a business-sustaining cost object and the other final cost objects. If and when these costs are assigned to final cost objects, organisations that do so often refer to them as a *management tax*, representing a cost of doing business apart from the products and service lines. If forced to fully absorb sustaining costs, the only fair way is to first assign and calculate all other cost objects and then use those cost results as the assignment basis. Like a rising tide lifts all boats, all cost objects are equitably charged with the tax.

Examples of final cost objects that comprise business-sustaining cost objects include senior management (at individual levels, such as headquarters, corporate, division and local) or government regulatory agencies (such as environmental, occupational safety or tax authorities). In effect, regulatory organisations (through their policies and compliance requirements) or executives (through their informal desires such as briefings or forecasts) place demands on work activities not caused by, or attributable to, specific products or customers.

Other categories of expenses that may be included as business-sustaining costs are idle, but available, capacity costs or research and development (R&D). R&D expenses might be optionally assigned into the business-sustaining costs so that the timing of the recognition of expenses is reasonably matched with turnover recognition for sales of the products or service lines. Because activity-based costing is management accounting, not regulated financial reporting, strict rules of generally accepted accounting principles do not need to be followed, however, they can be borrowed.

THE TWO VIEWS OF COSTS: THE ASSIGNMENT VIEW VERSUS THE PROCESS VIEW

Substantial confusion exists between the costs of processes and output costing (eg, product costs), even by accountants. Let's clarify the differences.

As earlier mentioned, ABC/M requires two separate cost assignment structures: (1) the horizontal process cost scheme governed by the time sequence of activities that belong to the various processes, and (2) the vertical cost re-assignment scheme governed by the variation and diversity of the cost objects. In effect, think of this vertical ABC/M cost assignment view as being time-blind. The ABC/M process costing view, at the activity stage, is blind to output mix. The cost assignment and business process costing are two different views of the same resource expenses and their activity costs. They are equivalent in amount, but the display of the information is radically different in each view.

Vertical Axis

The vertical axis, as illustrated in Figure 6-2, reflects costs that are sensitive to demands from all forms of product, channel and customer diversity and variety. The work activities consume the resources, and the products and customer services consume the work activities. The ABC/M cost assignment view is a cost-consumption chain. When each cost is traced based on its unique quantity or proportion of its driver, all the resource expenses are eventually re-aggregated into the final cost objects. This method provides much more accurate measures of product, channel and customer costs than the traditional and arbitrary, broadly averaged cost allocation method without causality.

Figure 6-2: The Vertical View of Assigning Costs

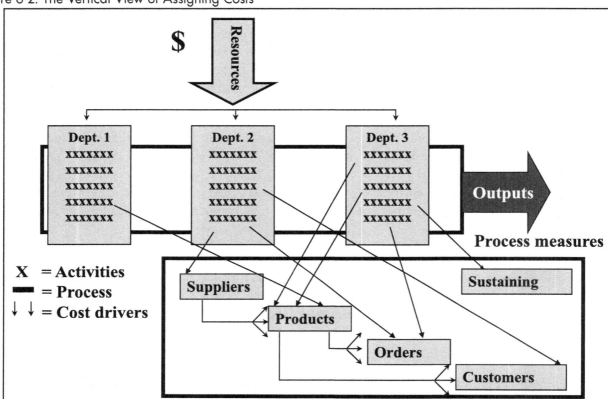

Source: Copyright Gary Cokins. Used with permission.

Horizontal Axis

The horizontal view, as illustrated in Figure 6-3, of activity costs represents the business process view. A *business process* can be defined as two or more activities, or a network of activities, with a common purpose. Activity costs belong to the business processes. Across each process, the activity costs are sequential and additive. In this orientation, activity costs satisfy the requirements for popular flow-charting (eg, swim lane diagrams) and process mapping and modelling techniques. Business process-based thinking can be visualised as tipping the organisation chart 90 degrees. ABC/M provides the activity cost elements for process costing that are not available from the general ledger.

Figure 6-3: The Horizontal View of Sequencing Costs

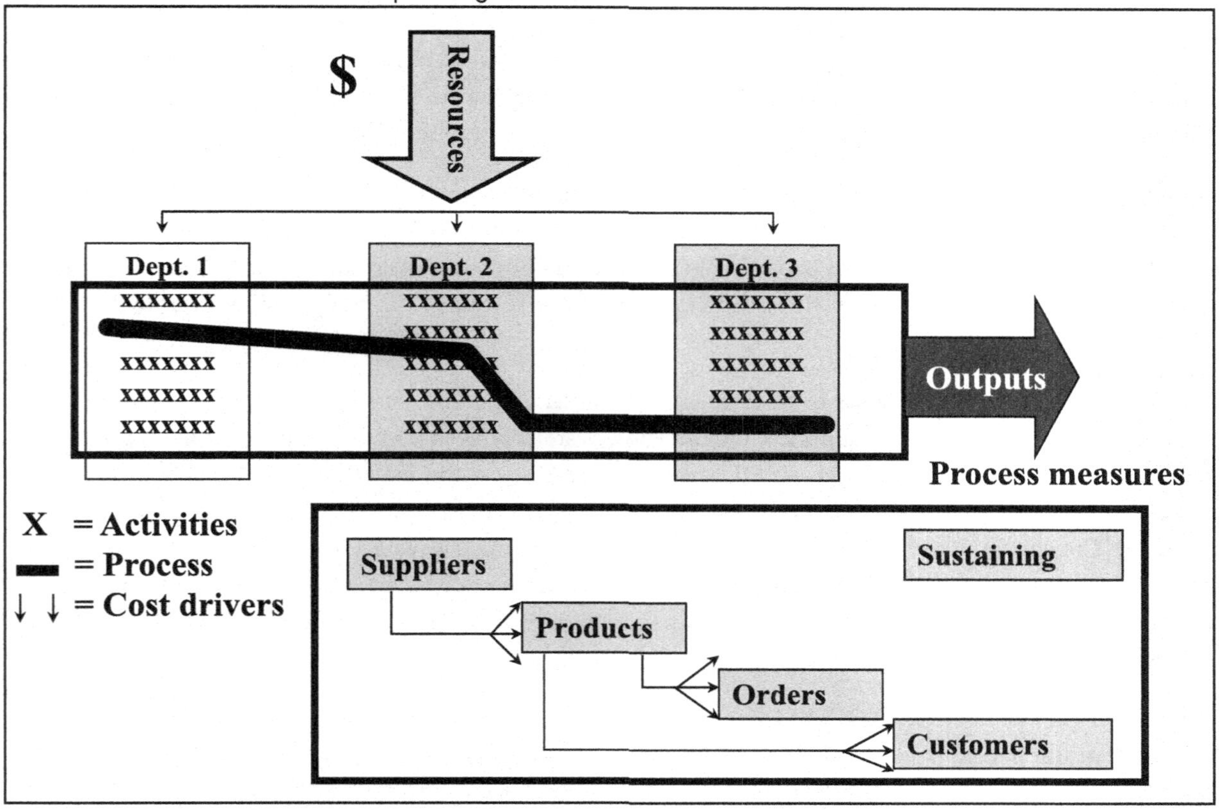

Source: Copyright Gary Cokins. Used with permission.

In summary, the vertical cost assignment view explains what specific things cost using their resource and activity drivers, whereas the horizontal process view illustrates how much processes cost.

HOW DOES ACTIVITY-BASED COSTING COMPUTE BETTER ACCURACIES?

When people who are first exposed to ABC/M hear the phrase, 'It is better to be approximately correct than precisely inaccurate,' they smile because they know exactly what that means in their organisation. However they usually do not know what causes ABC/M to produce substantially better accuracy relative to their existing legacy costing system despite ABC/M's abundant use of estimates and approximations. One of the explanations, which is counter-intuitive to many, is that the initial errors from resource driver estimates in an ABC/M assignment system cancel out. This is due, in part, because allocating (ie, re-assigning expenses into costs) is a closed system with a zero sum total error in the total costs of the final cost objects. Every assignment normalises to 100%, and any errors offset and cancel out. This is ABC/M's activity cost error dampening effect.

The starting amount of expenses to be traced and assigned can be assumed to be 100.000% accurate because they come from the general ledger accounting system (or source payroll and purchasing data sources) that is specially designed to accumulate and summarise the detailed spending transactions. However, subsequently, as we re-assign expenses into calculated costs, imprecise inputs do not automatically result in inaccurate outputs. That is, precision is not synonymous with accuracy. On the surface this is counter-intuitive. In ABC/M's cost assignment view, estimating error does not compound, it dampens out. These are properties of statistics found in equilibrium networks (ie, the amount of expenses and costs remains constant through the cost flow network), and ABC/M is a cost re-assignment network much more than it is an accounting system.

Even more startling is that the cost assignment network structure itself is an even greater determinant that influences accuracy because each assignment path is detecting only the cost objects for which a consumption relationship exits. Compare that with broadly averaged cost allocations that disproportionately charge every cost object. (Remember the example of splitting the bill at the restaurant in the previous chapter?) The lesson is that costing is modelling.

In ABC/M, poor model design leads to poor results. A well-known and painful lesson about activity-based costing is that when an ABC/M system implementation system falls short of its expectations, it is often because the system was over-engineered in size and detail. The ABC/M system usually quickly reached diminishing returns in extra accuracy for incremental levels of effort, but this effect was not recognised by the ABC/M project team. The system was built so large in size that the administrative effort to collect the data and maintain the system was ultimately judged to be not worth the perceived benefits. This results in a 'death by details' ABC/M project. It is unsustainable. In short, over-designed ABC/M systems are too detailed relative to their intended use.

As the designers construct their ABC/M information system, they usually suffer from a terrible case of lack of depth perception. There is no perspective from which they can judge how high or low or summarised or detailed they are. The implementation of an ABC/M system is usually influenced by accountants, and an accountant's natural instincts include a 'lowest common denominator mentality.' Accountants usually assume a detailed and comprehensive level of data collection based on the premise that if you collect a great amount of detail everywhere, from everybody, and about everything they do, you can then summarise anywhere. This is a 'just in case' approach in anticipation of any future, remote questions. The term *accuracy requirements* is apparently not in many accountants' vocabulary. As a result, their ABC/M models tend to become excessively large. They may ultimately become unmaintainable and not sustainable. Eventually the ABC/M system does not appear to be worth the effort. I am not criticising or attacking accountants. Years of training reinforce their high need for precision. However, ABC/M requires a bias towards practical use of the data.

The illusion that more detailed and granular data provide higher accuracy is part of the explanation for this behaviour. Another explanation for oversized ABC/M models is that at the outset of an ABC/M project, it is nearly impossible to pre-determine what levels of detail to go to. There are so many interdependencies in an ABC/M model that, as a result, it presents a problem. It is almost impossible to perform one of the earlier steps of a traditional IT function's systems development project plan—defining data requirements.

As an example, a question frequently asked by organisations implementing activity-based costing is, 'How many activities should be included in an activity-based costing system?' There is no correct answer because the number of activities is dependent on the answer to several other questions, such as, 'What problem are you trying to solve with the activity-based costing data?' In other words, the size, depth, granularity and accuracy of an activity-based costing system are dependent variables determined by other factors. The level of detail and accuracy of an activity-based costing system depends on what decisions the data will be used for. Implementing an ABC/M system with rapid prototyping, a technique that quickly resolves this problem, is discussed later in this chapter.

What is missing in most ABC/M implementations is a good understanding of what factors actually determine the accuracy of the ABC/M-calculated outputs. That is, what are the major determinants of higher accuracy of final cost objects? The following assertion will likely be counter-intuitive, not only to accountants, but also to everyone who designs and builds ABC/M systems. As earlier mentioned, ABC/M's substantially improved accuracy relative to traditional approaches actually resides more in the ABC/M cost assignment network structure itself than in the activity costs and the activity driver quantities. That is, the reason that the products, service lines, channels and customer costs are so reasonably accurate has less to do with their driver input data than with the architecture of the cost flow paths that make up the ABC/M cost assignment network.

Achieving success with ABC/M initially begins with overcoming the ABC/M levelling problem—right-sizing the model to a proper level of detail and disaggregation. Once the appropriate levels are stabilised at a Goldilocks level (ie, not too detailed nor too summarised), then the connection of the ABC/M data to business problems, their analysis and ultimate solutions can follow. In the end, the payback from implementing ABC/M can be accelerated.

ACTIVITY-BASED MANAGEMENT RAPID PROTOTYPING: GETTING QUICK AND ACCURATE RESULTS

The ABC/M levelling problem can be partly solved using the increasingly popular technique of *ABC/M rapid prototyping*. This is a method of building the first ABC/M model in a few short days, relying on knowledgeable employees, followed by a few weeks of iterative re-modelling to gradually, but not excessively, scale up the size of the model. Its benefits are accelerated learning and right-sizing the ABC/M model. In addition to this highly managed trial and error approach, effective levelling of the ABC/M model can be achieved through better thinking. Figure 6-4 illustrates ABC/M iterative re-modelling.

Figure 6-4: Rapid Prototyping with Iterative Remodelling.
Each iteration enhances the use of the ABC/M system.

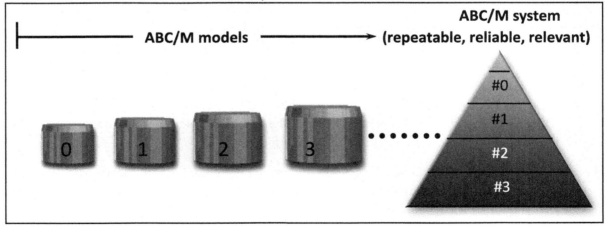

In a closed cost assignment system, there is a zero sum error, and error dampens out into cost objects. Figure 6-5 shows several asymptotic curves that all have the same ultimate destination: perfectly accurate costs of cost objects (especially final cost objects), in which the accuracy level is represented by the vertical axis. The horizontal axis represents *the level of administrative effort* to collect, calculate and report the data. As previously explained, for each incremental level of effort to collect more and better data, there is proportionately less improvement in accuracy. The asymptotic curves reflect both the error-dampening effect of offsetting activity cost error and improved design of the cost assignment network structure.

Figure 6-5: Balancing Levels of Accuracy With Effort

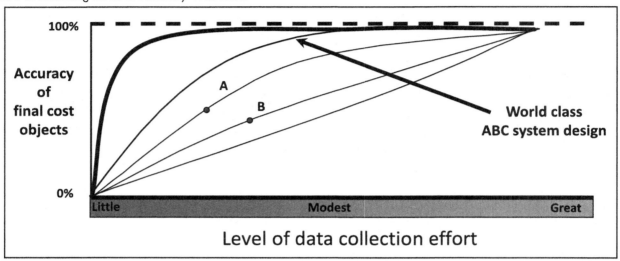

Source: Copyright Gary Cokins. Used with permission.

The question 'Is the climb worth the view?' is applicable to ABC/M. That is, by building a more detailed and slightly more accurate ABC/M model, will the answer to your question be better answered? Avoid the creeping elegance syndrome, ie the tendency to add details at the expense of the basic design. Larger models introduce maintenance issues. ABC/M rapid prototyping accelerates a team's understanding and acceptance of ABC/M by quickly giving them a vision of what their completed ABC/M system will look like—once scaled to its proper level of detail—and how they will use the new ABC/M information.

PRODUCT PROFITABILITY ANALYSIS

Because the product costs from ABC/M will be different compared to the costs from the existing, broadly-averaged and non-causal relationship method, and the selling prices are unaffected, product profits will also be different. They have to be different. It is simple math. The top line sales minus the middle line costs equals profit. Profit is a derivative of the first two lines in the equation.

Because analysis is expanding beyond product standard service line profitability to include channels and customers, the next chapter will discuss all the profit contribution layers.

TWO ALTERNATIVE EQUATIONS FOR COSTING ACTIVITIES AND COST OBJECTS

Two alternative approaches exist for computing activity costs and the costs of cost objects, such as products. The two approaches differ based on which data one prefers to collect versus calculate and how your organisation prefers to use feedback data to control its costs. The two approaches are as follows:

- *Activity driver equations.* First, activity costs are derived (via surveys, timesheets, estimates, etc). Then the quantity, frequency or intensity of the activity driver is collected per each activity. A unit cost rate per each activity driver is computed and then applied to all the cost objects based on their unique quantity of the activity driver events (eg, number of invoices processed). This is re-calculated for each time period for each work activity.

- *Cost object equations.* This approach begins with an in-depth time measurement study of work tasks and processes. It is the basis for time-driven ABC. In the study, the per unit time element for various (and optional) processing steps for each product (or product group) and each type of order are surveyed with deep time studies. Then each product and type of order is profiled with an equation specifying the sum of the number of transactions (eg, events) for each product or type of order. Finally, the quantity of the products and order types is counted for the period and backflushed against each product's or order's standard minutes-per-event to calculate an activity cost. This activity cost assumes the standard rate and is not the actual activity costs. The premise that this assumption is acceptable is that micro-measured activities do not vary much over time. What drives requirements for expenses is the varying mix and volume of products and type of orders.

Both approaches are intended to compute profitability margins for products, order types and, ideally, for channels and customer types as well. Each approach arrives at comparable answers in different ways. With regard to operational control and feedback, the two approaches are different because of which data each approach collects and computes. The *activity driver equation approach* monitors trends in activity driver cost rates, and it can be used to calculate and report cost variances to monitor efficiencies. It consequently focuses on activity performance. In contrast, the *cost object equation approach* attempts to provide information about the magnitude of idle capacity (primarily number of employees), so this approach focuses more on usage levels of resources and less on activity performance.

Figure 6-6 displays where these two approaches are located with respect to the ABC/M cost assignment network and how they differ. The activity driver equation approach solves for cost of the cost objects based on measuring or estimating activity costs and tracing them per events (ie, activity driver quantities). In contrast, the cost object equation approach begins with product and order type profiles, collects volume and mix data, and then solves for the activity costs, assuming the standard times are correct and incurred. It starts with a low level of characteristics of the cost object. This approach appears to reverse-calculate to determine the activity costs.

Figure 6-6: Two Cost Equation Approaches.

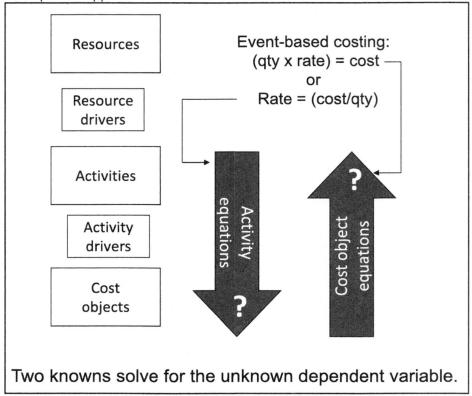

Source: Copyright Gary Cokins. Used with permission.

In practice, for historical reporting, there is no proper direction of flow of costs. Costing is modelling, and historical costs are like an electric circuit—it is a directionless transformation of expenses into costs. So both of these equation-based costing methods are in synchronisation. They simply arrive at a similar answer using different assumptions. (However, for predictive costing, which is a separate topic, direction of flow is from outputs placing demands on work that then draw on resource capacity. Predictive costing uses historical ABC/M as its foundation but includes many more assumptions.)

For the activity driver equation approach, you solve for the activity driver rate by assuming that data for the other two factors can be collected or reasonably estimated. For the cost object equation approach, you solve for the activity cost, at a standard cost, by presuming that processing times for each product's (ie, output) characteristics have been measured, profiles for each product configured, and then the product mix volumes are reported. The superior ABC/M software can compute costs in both directions.

Regardless of which equation-based approach is used, be cautious to first recognise the primary reasons you may be pursuing ABC/M data. Then, presuming there will be some interest in using the ABC/M for operational cost control and feedback, be clear in what type of feedback costs you will be more interested.

Part 3

STRATEGY MANAGEMENT

'A man's mind stretched by a new idea can never go back
to its original dimensions.'
—Oliver Wendell Holmes,
U.S. Supreme Court Justice, 1897

7

THE PROMISE AND PERILS OF THE BALANCED SCORECARD

The balanced scorecard, the methodology developed by Drs. Robert S. Kaplan and David Norton, recognises the shortcomings of executive managements' excessive emphasis on after the fact, short-term financial results. It resolves this myopia and improves organisational performance by shifting attention from financial measures and managing non-financial operational measures to customers, internal processes, and employee innovation, learning and growth. These influencing measures are reported during the period when reactions can occur sooner, which in turn, leads to better financial results.

The balanced scorecard is one of the underpinnings needed to complete the full vision of the performance management framework. Will the adoption rate of the balanced scorecard find the same difficulty crossing the chasms encountered by activity-based cost management (ABC/M) systems in the 1990s? It took many failures in ABC/M system implementations before organisations learned what ABC/M is and how to shape, size and level the detail of ABC/M systems before organisations began to get them ready for use. Are balanced scorecard implementations going to experience the same difficulty?

WHAT IS A BALANCED SCORECARD?

An early indication of trouble is the confusion about what a balanced scorecard is and more confusion about what its purpose is. There is little consensus. If you ask executives whether they are using a balanced scorecard, many say they are. However, if you next ask them to describe it, you'll get widely different descriptions. There is no standard — yet. Some executives say they have successfully transferred their old columnar management reports into visual dashboards with flashing red and green lights and directional arrows. Some realise a scorecard is more than that, and they have compressed their old measures into a smaller, more manageable number of more relevant measures. Neither may be the correct method.

How does anyone know if those measures—the so-called 'key performance indicators' (KPIs)—support the strategic intent of the executive team? Are the selected measures the right measures? Or are they what you can measure rather than what you should measure? Is the purpose of the scorecard only to better monitor the dials, rather than facilitate the employee actions needed to move the dials?

Discussion about balanced scorecards and dashboards is regularly appearing in business magazines, website discussion groups and at conferences. Today's technology makes it relatively simple to convert reported data into a dashboard dial, but what are the consequences? What actions are suggested from just monitoring the dials?

In Chapter 4, 'A Taxonomy of Accounting and Costing Methods,' I said that results and outcome information should answer three questions: What? So what? and Then what? These same questions apply here. Sadly, most scorecards and dashboards only answer the first question. Worse yet, answering the 'what' may not even focus on a relevant 'what.' Organisations struggle with determining what to measure.

Organisations need to think deeper about what measures drive value and reflect achieving the direction-setting strategic objectives of their executive team. With the correct measures, organisations should strive to optimise these measures and ideally be continuously forecasting their expected results.

Balanced Scorecards Are Companions to Strategy Maps

Why are so many people familiar with the term *balanced scorecard* but so few are familiar with the term *strategy maps*? I believe the strategy map is orders of magnitude more important than the scorecard, which is merely a feedback mechanism. Why do executives want a balanced scorecard but without a strategy map? One possible explanation is the mistaken belief that those vital few KPI measures, rather than the trivial many, can be derived without first requiring employee teams and managers to understand the answer to a key question: Where does the executive team want the organisation to go? This question is best answered by the executive team's vision and mission—and they must point in the direction they want the organisation to go. That is the executive team's primary job—setting direction. The strategy map and its companion balance scorecard are also important, but their combination answers a different question: How will we get there?

Figure 7-1 illustrates a generic strategy map with its four stacked, popular perspectives. Each rectangle represents a strategic objective and its associated projects, processes or competencies at which to excel plus their appropriate measures and targets.

Figure 7-1: Generic Strategy Map Architecture

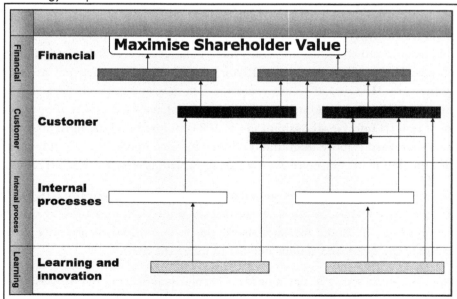

Note that there are dependency linkages in a strategy map with an upward direction of cumulating effects of contributions. The derived KPIs are not in isolation but, rather, have context to the mission and vision. To summarise, a strategy maps linkages from the bottom perspective upward, which does the following:

- Accomplishing the employee innovation, learning and growth objectives contributes to the internal process improvement objectives.

- Accomplishing the internal process objectives contributes to the customer satisfaction and loyalty objectives.

- Accomplishing the customer-related objectives results in achieving the financial objectives, typically a combination of turnover growth and cost management objectives.

The strategy map is like a force field in physics, as with magnetism, where the energy, priorities and actions of people are mobilised, aligned and focused. One can say that at the top of the map, maximising shareholder wealth (or for public sector organisations, maximising community and citizen value) is not really a goal—it is a result. It is a result of accomplishing all the linked strategic objectives with cause and effect relationships.

The peril that threatens the success of this methodology is executive teams that are anxious to assign measures with targets to employees and hold them accountable. Executives typically skip two critical steps of involving employees to gain their buy-in (and also commitment to the measures) to assure they understand the executive team's strategy, and the more critical prior step of identifying the mission-essential projects and initiatives that will achieve the strategic objectives. The presence of enabling projects and initiatives goes to the heart of what distinguishes a strategic objective from just getting better at what you have already been doing.

Figure 7-2 illustrates who ideally should be responsible for one of five elements of each strategic objective: the executive team or the managers and employees. Sadly, many organisations neglect the first two elements identified in a strategy map. They begin with the third column to select KPIs without constructing a strategy map. The enterprise practice management (EPM) intelligence resides in the strategy map.

Figure 7-2: Who is Responsible for What?
A scorecard is more of a social tool than a technical tool.

Measurement period	1st quarter					
	Strategic objective	Identify projects, initiatives or processes	KPI measure	KPI target	KPI actual	Comments/ explanation
Executive team	X	↕	↕	X		
Managers and employees		X	X		*Their score*	X
					<----- Period results ----->	

Source: Copyright Gary Cokins. Used with permission.

Strategy maps and their derived balanced scorecard are navigational tools to guide the organisation to implement the strategy, not necessarily to formulate the strategy. Executive teams are pretty good at defining strategy, but a high involuntary CEO turnover rate and the increasingly shorter tenure of CEOs are evidence of their failure to implement their strategy.

Measurements Are More of a Social System Than a Technical One

Do not misinterpret what I am saying. Selecting and measuring KPIs are critical. You get what you measure, and strategy maps and scorecards serve a greater social purpose than a technical one (although IT and software are essential enablers). Performance measures motivate people and focus them on what matters most.

Imagine if every day, every employee in an organisation, from the janitor to the CEO could answer the question 'How am I doing on what is important?' The first half of the question can be easily displayed on a dial with a target. It is reported in a scorecard or dashboard. However it is the second half of the question that is the key—'on what is important'—and that is defined from the strategy map.

The risk and peril of the balanced scorecard involves the process of identifying and integrating appropriate cause and effect linkages of strategic objectives that are each supported by the vital few measures and then subsequently cascading the KPIs down through the organisation. KPIs ultimately extend into performance indicators (PIs)—operational performance indicators—that employees can relate to and directly affect.

The primary task of a strategy map and its companion balanced scorecard is to align people's work and priorities with multiple strategic objectives that, if accomplished, will achieve the strategy and consequently realise the end-game of maximising shareholder wealth (or maximising citizen value). The strategic objectives are located in the strategy map, not in the balanced scorecard. The KPIs in the balanced scorecard reflect the strategic objectives in the strategy map.

Debate will continue about how to select the vital few KPIs for workgroups. The following are two approaches:

1. Newtonian-style managers, who believe the world is a big machine with dials, pulleys and levers to push and pull, find appeal in looking at benchmark data to identify which relevant and unfavourably large performance gaps they should focus on. They want to know, 'What must we get better at?' The KPIs are then derived, and strategies are deduced from recognising deficiencies.

2. In contrast, Darwinian-style managers, who believe the organisation is a sense-and-respond organism, find appeal in having the executive team design the strategy map by applying a SWOT (strengths, weaknesses, opportunities and threats) approach. This approach begins with the executive team freely brainstorming and recording an organisation's SWOTs. They then cluster similar, individual SWOTs into strategic objectives with causal linkages in the strategy map. Following this initial step, the middle managers and core process owners are then tasked with identifying the few and manageable projects and core processes to improve that will attain the executive team's strategic objectives in the strategy map. After that step, those same middle managers can identify the KPIs that will indicate progress toward achieving the projects and improving critical core processes. This latter approach not only assures that middle managers and employee teams will understand the executive's strategy, of which most middle managers and employees are typically unaware, but it further generates their buy-in and ownership of the balanced scorecard's KPIs because these have not been mandated to them from the executives. (Of course, the executive team can subsequently challenge and revise their lower managers' selected projects and KPIs [debate is always healthy] but only after the buy-in and learning has occurred.)

SCORECARD OR REPORT CARD? THE IMPACT OF SENIOR MANAGEMENT'S ATTITUDE

Regardless of which technique or other method is used to identify the KPIs, the KPIs ideally should reflect the executive team's strategic intent and not be reported in isolation, as the annual financial budget typically is disconnected from the strategy. This is the peril of the balanced scorecard. Its main purpose is to communicate the executive team's strategy to employees in a way they can understand and to report the impact of their contribution to attaining it. However starting with a KPI definition without context to the executive's mission and vision denies this important step.

Research from a former State University of New York, Albany Professor, Raef Lawson, suggests that a major differentiator of success from failure in a balanced scorecard implementation is the senior management's attitude. Is it a scorecard or report card? Will we use it for punishment or remedy? Do we work for bosses we must 'obey?' Or do we work for coaches, like on a sports team, and mentors who guide and advise us?

As an example, is senior management anxiously awaiting those dashboards so they can follow the cascading score meters downward in order to micro-manage the workers under their middle managers? Or will the executives appropriately restrict their primary role and responsibility to define and continuously adjust strategy (which is dynamic, not static, always reacting to new insights) and then allow the empowerment of employee teams to select KPIs from which employees can actively determine the corrective interventions to align with the strategy?

The superior strategy map and scorecard systems embrace employee teams that communicate among themselves to take action, rather than a supervisory command-and-control style from senior managers. An executive team micro-managing the KPI score performance of employees can be harsh. If the strategy map and cascading KPI and PI selection exercise is done well and subsequently maintained, then higher level managers need only view their own score performance, share their results with the employee teams below them and coach the teams to improve their KPI and PI scores or re-consider adding or deleting KPIs or PIs. For the more mature, balanced scorecard users using commercial software, they can re-adjust the KPI and PI weighting coefficients to steer toward better alignment with the strategic objectives.

GPS NAVIGATORS FOR AN ORGANISATION

In Chapter 2, 'Enterprise Performance Management: Myth or Reality?' I described a car analogy in which the latest thing is to have a global positioning system (GPS) route navigator in our car. As with most new technologies, such as when handheld calculators replaced slide rules or laptop computers emerged, a GPS is another gadget that is evolving into a necessity. They get you to your destination, and a comforting voice guides you along the way. Why can't an organisation have a similar device? It can.

My belief is the refinement in usage of strategy maps and its companion balanced scorecard is becoming the GPS route navigator for organisations. For organisations, the destination input into the GPS is the executive team's strategy. As earlier described, the executive team's primary job is to set strategic direction, and the top of their strategy map is their destination. However, unlike a GPS's knowledge of roads and algorithms to determine the best route, managers and employee teams must 'map' which projects, initiatives and business process improvements are best to get to the destination for realising the strategy. In addition, when you are driving a car with a GPS instrument and you make a wrong turn, the GPS's voice tells you that you are off track—and it then provides you with a corrective action instruction. However with most organisation's calendar-based and long cycle-time reporting, there is delayed reaction. The EPM framework includes a GPS.

Next, the organisation as the car itself needs to be included. The motor and driveshaft are the employees, with their various methodologies, such as customer value management and service delivery, that propel the organisation toward its target. Collectively, the many methodologies, including lean management and activity-based costing, constitute performance management as the organisation's gears.

Just like a poorly performing car with some broken gears, misaligned tires and poor lubrication will yield poor gallons per mile (or litres per kilometre), poorly integrated methodologies, impure raw data and lack of digitisation and analytics results in poor rate of shareholder financial wealth creation. The full vision of EPM removes the friction and vibration plus weak torque to not only optimise the consumption of the organisation's resources—its employees and spending—but it also gets the organisation to its strategy destination better, faster, cheaper, smarter and safer. The result? A higher shareholder wealth creation yield?

Finally, as earlier mentioned, a strategy is never static but is constantly adjusted. It is dynamic, which means the destination input to the GPS navigator is constantly changing. This places increasing importance on predictive analytics to determine where the best destination for stakeholders is located. How much longer do you want to drive your existing car when an EPM car with a GPS is now available to lift wealth creation efficiency and yield?

Some proposed management improvement methodologies, like the lights-out, fully automated manufacturing factory touted in the 1980s, are fads that come and go, but the strategy map and its companion, the balanced scorecard for feedback, are certain to be a sustained methodology in the long term—perhaps forever. It makes sense that executive teams provide direction-setting, and employee teams then perform the actions to get there. Are these early 21st century missteps and misunderstandings in implementing the balanced scorecard due to arrogance, ignorance or inexperience? I suggest it is due to inexperience.

Conflict and tension are natural in all organisations. Therefore, it takes managers and employees time to stabilise what ultimately is a behavioural measurement mechanism of cause and effect KPIs to distinguish between KPIs and PIs and to then master how to use both these types of measures to navigate, power and steer as an integrated enterprise. As stated by the author Peter Senge, a thought leader in the field of organisational change management, the differentiator between successful and failing organisations will be the rate, and not just the amount, of organisational learning. Those intangible assets—employees as knowledge workers and the information provided to them—are what truly power the EPM framework.

HOW ARE BALANCED SCORECARDS AND DASHBOARDS DIFFERENT?

Confusion exists about the difference between a balanced scorecard and a dashboard. There is similar confusion differentiating KPIs from normal and routine measures that we refer to as PIs. The word 'key' in KPI is the operative term. When an organisation proudly proclaims they have 300 KPIs, one must ask them the question, how can they all be key?

An organisation has only so many supplies or energy to focus. To use a radio analogy, KPIs are what distinguish the signal from the noise—the measures of progress toward strategy implementation. As a negative result of this confusion, organisations are including an excessive amount of PIs in their balanced scorecard that should be restricted only to KPIs.

A misconception about a balanced scorecard is that its primary purpose is to monitor results. That is secondary. Its primary purposes are to report the carefully selected measures that reflect the strategic intent of the executive team and then enable ongoing understanding about what should be done to align the organisation's work and priorities to attain the executive team's strategic objectives. The strategic objectives should ideally be articulated in a strategy map, which serves as the visual vehicle from which to identify the projects and initiatives needed to accomplish each objective or the specific core processes at which the organisation needs to excel. After this step is completed, KPIs are selected, and their performance targets are set. With this understanding, it becomes apparent that the strategy map's companion scorecard, on its surface, serves more as a feedback mechanism to allow everyone in the organisation, from front-line workers up to the executive team, to answer that previously posed question, 'How are we doing on what is important?' More importantly, the scorecard should facilitate analysis to also know why. The idea is not to just monitor the dials but to move the dials.

Michael Hammer, the author who introduced the concept of business process re-engineering, described the sad situation of measurement abuse in his book, *The Agenda: What Every Business Must Do to Dominate the Decade*:

> In the real world ... a company's measurement systems typically deliver a blizzard of nearly meaningless data that quantifies practically everything in sight, no matter how unimportant; that is devoid of any particular rhyme or reason; that is so voluminous as to be unusable; that is delivered so late as to be virtually useless; and that then languishes in printouts and briefing books without being put to any significant purpose.... In short, measurement is a mess.... We measure far too much and get far too little for what we measure because we never articulated what we need to get better at, and our measures aren't tied together to support higher-level decision making.[1]

Hammer did not hide his feelings, but has the cure been worse than the ailment? Simply reducing the number of measures can still result in an organisation measuring what it can measure as opposed to what it should measure. To determine what you should measure requires deeper understanding of the underlying purposes of a balanced scorecard relative to a dashboard.

Scorecards and Dashboards Serve Different Purposes

The two terms—*scorecards* and *dashboards*—have a tendency to confuse or, rather, get used interchangeably, when each brings a different set of capabilities. The sources of the confusion are as follows:

- Both represent a way to track results.
- Both make use of traffic light colouring systems, dials, sliders and other visual aids.
- Both can have targets, thresholds and alert messages.
- Both can provide drill down to other measurements and reports.

The difference comes from the context in which they are applied. To provide some history, as busy executives and managers have struggled to keep up with the amount of information being thrust at them, the concept of 'traffic lighting' has been applied to virtually any and all types of reporting. As technology has improved, more features have been added. An example is the ability to link to other reports and to drill down to finer levels of detail. The common denominator was the speed of being able to focus on something that required action or further investigation. The terminology evolved to reflect how technology vendors described what provided this capability. As a consequence, both dashboard and scorecard terms are being used interchangeably.

Figure 7-3 illustrates the difference between scorecards and dashboards, starting with all measurements as their source. Scorecards and dashboards are not contradictory. They both display measurement, and they are both important, but they serve different purposes.

Figure 7-3: Strategic KPI Scorecards Versus PI Dashboards

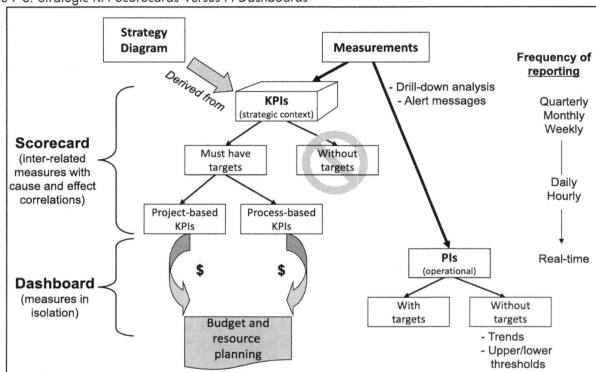

Source: Copyright Gary Cokins. Used with permission.

The top of the figure is the realm of scorecards. Scorecards are intended to be strategic. They align the behaviour of employees and partners with the strategic objectives formulated by the executive team. In contrast, dashboards, at the bottom of the figure, are intended to be operational.

Some refer to dashboards as 'dumb' reporting and scorecards as 'intelligent' reporting. The reason is that dashboards primarily are for data visualisation. They display what is happening during a time period. Most organisations begin with identifying what they are already measuring and construct a dashboard dial from there. However, dashboards do not communicate why something matters, why someone should care about the reported measure or what the impact may be if an undesirable declining measure continues. In short, dashboards report what you can measure.

In contrast, a scorecard does provide the information lacking in dashboards. A scorecard additionally answers questions by providing deeper analysis, drill-down capabilities, traffic light alert messaging and forecasting for inferences of performance potential to determine motivational targets. Scorecards do not start with the existing data but, rather, they begin with identifying what strategic projects to complete and core processes to improve and excel in.

The selection and validation of the correct or best KPIs is a constant debate. Statistical correlation interaction analysis among KPIs can determine the degree of influence and 'lift' that various cascaded KPIs have on the higher level, enterprise-wide KPIs. Hence, correlation analysis validates or improves the KPI selection. In addition, this type of analysis can automatically uncover previously unknown statistical relationships that may suggest cause and effects and can be used for predictive power. You want to make changes based on anticipated targets and constantly refocused outcomes so that employees can proactively make changes before unexpected events occur that would require a much more expensive reaction. In short, scorecards report what you should measure.

The following are some guidelines for understanding the differences:[2]

- *Scorecards monitor progress toward accomplishing strategic objectives.* A scorecard displays periodic snapshots of performance associated with an organisation's strategic objectives and plans. It measures organisational activity at a summary level against pre-defined targets to see if performance is within acceptable ranges. Its selection of KPIs helps executives communicate strategy to employees and focuses users on the highest priority projects, initiatives, actions and tasks required to implement plans. The word 'key' differentiates KPIs from the PIs reported in dashboards.

  Scorecard KPIs ideally should be derived from a strategy map, rather than just a list of important measures that the executives have requested to be reported. Regardless of whether the suggested Kaplan and Norton four-stacked perspectives, or some variant, are used, scorecard KPIs should have cause and effect linkages (eg, statistical correlations). Directionally upward from the employee-centric innovation, learning and growth perspectives, the KPIs should reveal the cumulative build of potential to realised economic value.

  There are two key distinctions of scorecards: (1) Each KPI must require a pre-defined target measure, and (2) KPIs should comprise both project-based KPIs (eg, milestones, progress percentage of completion, degree of planned versus accomplished outcome) and process-based KPIs (eg, customer satisfaction, % on-time delivery against customer promise dates). A scorecard comprising mainly or exclusively process-based KPIs is not an efficient engine of change. It merely monitors whether progress from the traditional drivers of improvement, such as quality or cycle-time improvement, is occurring. Process improvement is important, but innovation and change is even more important. Strategy is all about change and not just doing the same things better.

- *Dashboards monitor and measure processes.* A dashboard, however, is operational and reports information typically more frequently than scorecards and usually with measures. Each dashboard measure is reported with little regard to its relationship to other dashboard measures. Dashboard measures do not directly reflect the context of strategic objectives.

  This information can be more real-time in nature, like a car dashboard that shows drivers their current speed, fuel level and engine temperature. A dashboard ideally should be directly linked to systems that capture events as they happen, and it should warn users through alerts or exception notifications when performance against any number of measurements deviates from the norm or what is expected.

I caution organisations that are paying more attention to their performance measurements about (1) the linkage of scorecard KPIs to the strategy map and also to the fiscal budget (as well as rolling financial forecasts), and

(2) the linkage of dashboard PIs selected to influence behaviour that will ultimately result in achieving or exceeding the KPI targets. Strategy diagrams and the budget are located in Figure 7-3 and are described in the following text.

Scorecards Link the Executives' Strategy to Operations and the Budget

A strategy diagram is located in the upper left of Figure 7-3. The figure denotes that KPIs should be derived from the executives' strategic objectives and plans. If KPIs are selected independent of the strategy, then they will likely report only what can be measured, as opposed to what should be measured. Failure to implement a strategy is one of a CEO's major concerns and, therefore, KPIs should either reflect mission-critical projects and initiatives or core business processes that must be excelled at. (Hence, there is the need for both project-based and process-based KPIs.)

The budget (and increasingly rolling financial forecasts) should be derived from the required funding of the projects (ie, the nonrecurring strategy expenses and capital investments) and the operational processes (ie, the recurring operational capacity-related expenses that vary with driver volumes, such as customer demand).

A strategy is dynamic and never static, as executives appropriately shift directions based on their new insights and observations. Reliably accurate forecasting is critical for both strategy formulation and future resource capacity management. Hence, both the KPIs and the necessary funding to realise the strategic plans will continuously be derived from the 'living' strategy diagram.

Dashboards Move the Scorecard's Dials

The organisation's traction and torque is reflected in the dashboard's PI measures—the more frequently reported operational measures. Although some PIs may have pre-defined targets, PIs serve more to monitor trends across time or results against upper or lower threshold limits. As PIs are monitored and responded to, then the corrective actions will contribute to achieving the KPI target levels with actual results.

Cause and effect relationships between and among measures underlie the entire approach to integrating the strategy map (formulation), balanced scorecard (appraisal), dashboards (implementation) and fiscal budgets (the fuel).

Strategy Is More Than Performing Better

A key to organisational survival involves differentiation from competitors. An important role of the executive team is to exhibit vision and constantly determine innovation to differentiate their organisation from others. This explains a misunderstanding about strategic objectives. Some mistakenly believe the purpose of strategic objectives is to keep an organisation adhered to a single, unbroken path. This is certainly not the case. As mentioned earlier, strategy is dynamic, not static. The purpose of strategic objectives in a strategy map is to re-direct the organisation from the tyranny of maintaining the status quo. Strategy is about constant change. If an organisation does not constantly change, then it is exposed to the competitors constantly converging to similar products, services and processes. Differentiation is key to maintaining a competitive edge. Strategic objectives are about the changes an organisation should make to maintain a competitive edge.

Dashboards and scorecards are not mutually exclusive. In fact, the best dashboards and scorecards merge elements from one another.

A simple rule is to use the term *dashboard* when you merely want to keep score, like during a sporting event, and use the term *scorecard* when you want to understand the context of key scores in terms of how they influence achievement of strategic outcomes. A scorecard's measures will be fewer in number—they are strategic and carry more weight and influence. In contrast, the number of dashboard measures could number in the hundreds or thousands—but you still need a way to focus on the unfavourable-to-target ones fast for tactical action. However, action with respect to a single measurement in a dashboard is less likely to change strategic outcomes as dramatically as compared to when reported in a scorecard.

In general, scorecard KPIs are associated with the domain of the performance management framework. In contrast, dashboard PIs are associated with business intelligence.

Getting Past the Speed Bumps

I believe that the balanced scorecard and dashboard components of commercial EPM software should have some, but not many, pre-defined KPIs. That is, the vendor's software should deliberately come with a limited, rather than a comprehensive, selection of KPIs that are commonly used by each type of industry. Otherwise, they will be used as a crutch without the deeper thinking. The same goes for websites with KPI dictionaries. The purpose of providing standard KPIs should only be to accelerate the implementation of an organisation's construction of their scorecard and dashboard system with a jump-start.

The reason for not providing a comprehensive and exhaustive list of industry-specific measures is because caution is needed whenever an organisation is identifying its measures. Measures drive employee behaviour. Caution is needed for two major reasons:

1. Measures should be tailored to an organisation's unique needs.
2. Organisations should understand the basic concepts that differentiate scorecards from dashboards and KPIs from PIs.

My interest is that organisations successfully implement and sustain an integrated strategic scorecard and operational dashboard system. Hence, organisations should understand the distinctions described here. This is why I caution against simply using a generic list of various industries' common KPIs and PIs, regardless of their source.

As with any improvement methodology, experience through use refines the methodology's effectiveness and impact. The 'plan-do-check-act' cycle is a great practice for learning organisations. With improvement methodologies, it is difficult to get it perfectly right the first time. There will always be a learning curve. Many organisations over-plan and under-implement. With regard to KPI and PI selection, first learn the principles and then apply them through selecting, monitoring and refining the KPIs. Strategy maps and balanced scorecards are a craft, not a science.

Endnotes

1 Hammer. Michael. *The Agenda: What Every Business Must Do to Dominate the Decade.* New York: Crown Business, 2001, p. 101.

2 Eckerson, Wayne W. *Performance Dashboards: Measuring, Monitoring, and Managing Your Business.* Hoboken, NJ: John Wiley & Sons, 2006, p. 8.

8

DESIGNING A STRATEGY MAP AND BALANCED SCORECARD

EIGHT STEPS TO CREATE A STRATEGY MAP

The steps for implementing a strategy map and its associated balanced scorecard are like a recipe. The initial steps for building the strategy map are primarily performed by the executive team. After that, the managers and employee teams get involved to identify the projects and initiatives and core processes needing improvement, all of which are intended to achieve the strategic objectives and identify the key performance indicators (KPIs). The steps are as follows:

1. First, agree on the vision, mission and strategic intent of the enterprise. Define the strategy.

The initial step is to define the organisation's vision and mission statements. These two statements are not the same, and their definitions must precede the construction of the strategy map and its associated scorecard and dashboards because they serve as signposts.

The vision statement answers the question 'Where do we want to go?' in terms that describe a highly desirable future state for the organisation. The statement should ideally be very brief, as the following examples demonstrate:

- Former U.S. President John F. Kennedy—'We will put a man on the moon.'
- Microsoft Corporation (1990s)—'A computer on every desk top.'
- Microsoft Corporation (21st century)—'Information anywhere, anytime.'
- The SAS Institute—'The Power to Know'

The mission statement provides to all employees the answer to the question, 'Why are we here?' in terms of desirable impacts to gain a competitive edge, such as

- to exceed customer needs well ahead of their realisation that they even have the need (eg, 24-hour automated teller machine).
- to leverage technology capabilities in fulfilling customer needs.
- to leverage employee capabilities for whatever we excel at.

Now the construction of the strategy map begins. Its initial purpose is to serve as a framework in the form of a network connecting strategic objectives, hence, the name *strategy map*.

2. Define the strategic objectives that support step 1.

Strategy maps (sometimes referred to as *value driver trees*) are used to communicate a unified view of the overarching strategy to the organisation. A strategy map defines corporate direction and aligns internal processes, strategic objectives, initiatives, KPI measures and target scores.

The balanced scorecard has received substantial attention, as if the scorecard was the answer, when, in fact, it is the strategy map that serves as a builder's blueprint for the scorecard. The strategy map is like the special ingredient in this recipe because its straightforward logic becomes so compelling. However at this point, the themes that blossom into strategic objectives have yet to be organised or positioned among themselves. That comes in the step 3.

3. Map the interrelated strategic objectives with their cause and effect linkages.

The strategic objectives are interrelated. The four perspectives, originally proposed in Kaplan and Norton's articles and books on the balanced scorecard, are very useful in simplifying what otherwise would be a difficult task. That task is to take all the strategic objectives (congealed from a workshop where the executives identify the strengths, weaknesses, opportunities and threats [SWOT] from the popular SWOT analysis and then cluster them into themes) and categorise each one into the perspectives it best fits.

The sequence of the four perspectives makes very good sense. The top perspective (ie, the financial perspective for commercial companies and the customer/stakeholder view for the public sector company) is the beneficiary of the strategic objectives in the three perspectives beneath it. The bottom perspective, the learning and growth (or enabling assets) perspective, is the most foundational, not unlike the foundation for a house.

An effective way to understand a strategy map is to visualise an example of a hypothetical one. Figure 8-1 illustrates a strategy map of hypothetical XYZ Corporation, where each node in the network represents a strategic objective. The figure further adds if-then linkages where the paths drive, or at least contribute to, the outcome of the strategic objectives above them.

An interesting question routinely asked is, 'Where is the organisation's strategy defined and located on the strategy map? The simple answer is it does not appear. Why? The reason is that the connected network of strategic objectives is equivalent to the strategy. Strategic objectives are the actions that an organisation must complete—or at least progress toward—to achieve the organisation's mission that, in turn, would realise its vision. The role of the strategy map is to show employees and managers what the organisation is looking for, rather than the executives questioning what they want the employees to do. In short, the strategic objectives, collectively, are the strategy.

Figure 8-1: XYZ Corporation Strategy Map

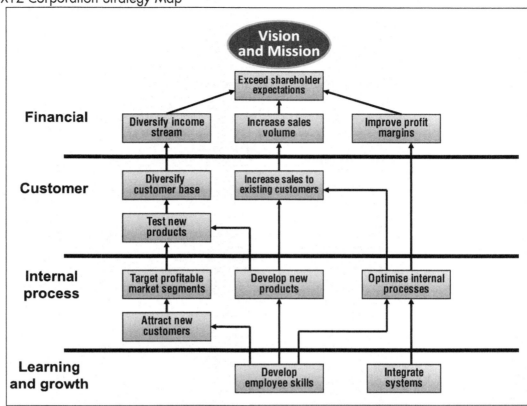

Source: Copyright Gary Cokins. Used with permission.

4. Define initiatives to close the performance gap for each strategic objective and scale back non-supportive projects.

Strategic objectives are oblique. You cannot go out there and 'do' an objective, but you can perform projects, programmes and actions or manage business processes that help accomplish the strategic objectives. In short, an effective performance management system demystifies the oblique strategic objectives by articulating how every action programme or business process—by teams and even individuals—contributes to the achievement of higher level enterprise strategic objectives and, subsequently, the vision and mission.

5. Select appropriate strategic measures and cascade them to relevant parts of the organisation.

A key in this step is to allow the different parts of the enterprise to define their own KPIs (tactical and operational measures), aimed at supporting the strategic KPIs and maintaining a shared focus on the strategy.

Up to this point, there have been no defined measures—specific or general. Now, they are defined. This is the most influential step for the success of the scorecard, yet is arguably the trickiest to perform.

Each strategic objective should be restricted to the KPI measures for the action programmes or business processes. A KPI should answer the question 'What is an excellent quantitative measure that would communicate how well the strategic objective is being accomplished?' by considering the action step or business process improvement aimed at the strategic objective. Do not confuse this step with choosing the specific target score for the KPI measure. That comes in step 7.

Figure 8-2 is the scorecard for the same hypothetical XYZ Company, whose strategy map can be viewed in Figure 8-1 in step 3. Note that strategic objectives are identical.

Figure 8-2: XYZ Corporation Balanced Scorecard

XYZ Corporation Balanced Scorecard

Vision: To be the premier provider of our products in specific global markets
Mission: To delight target customers through innovative products and application of leading-edge technology of our processes

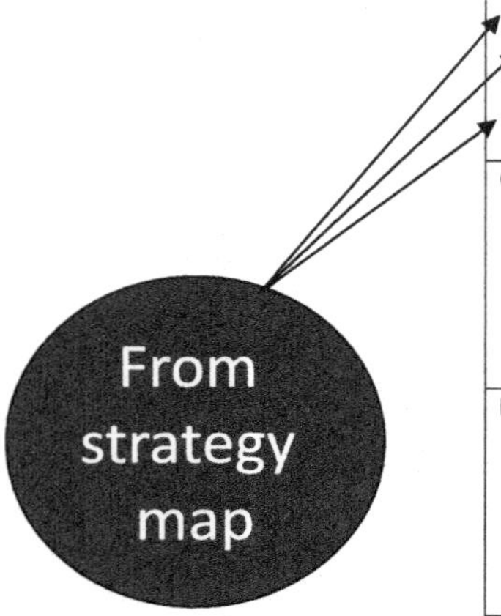

PERSPECTIVE/ Strategic Objectives	Lagging KPI Measures < --- <--- Leading KPI Measures	KPI Target	2Q, 200X KPI Actual	KPI score * >1, good <1, poor	Comments/ Explanation
FINANCIAL					
Exceed shareholder expectations	Share price	72.0	71.0	0.975	
	ROI	25.0%	21.5%		
40% Increase sales volume	Turnover ($ mil)	$6.000	$5.482		
35% Improve profit margins	Gross margin %	35.0%	31.6%		
	Operating expense % sales	20.0%	24.2%		
25% Diversify income stream	% $ from top 20% of customers	50%	48%		
	# products > 5% of turnover	6	7		
CUSTOMER					
Increase sales to	Cross-sell ratio %	30%	13%		
existing customers	Customer retention rate	95%	90%		
	% preferred supplier to	35%	20%		
Diversify customer base	# sales call to new markets	90	84		
Attract new customers	Revenues from new customers	$0.500	$0.800		
	advertising $ spent	$ 25.0 K	$ 23.4 K		
PROCESS					
Target profitable Customer segments	# segments identified	3	0		
Develop new products	Revenues from new products	$ 40.0 K	$ 55.5 K		
	New product intro time (# days)	60 days	95 days		
Streamline order	Fulfilment cycle time (#days)	7.5 days	8.8 days		
fullfillment process	On-time delivery %	95%	51%		
LEARNING AND GROWTH					
Develop employee skills	Profit per employee	$ 50.0 K	$ 32.5 K		
	Employee satisfaction index	80%	82%		
	# training days/employee	2.00	1.25		
	Retention rate	95%	99%		
Integrate systems	% IT plan integration	80%	90%		
	% orders received via Internet	10%	4%		

From strategy map (arrows pointing to 40%, 35%, 25% objectives)

* Score equation example: Share price		
	High:	92
	Low:	52
	Score = 1 + [(actual -target) / (high – low)] where high/low range has target as midpoint	

Source: Copyright Gary Cokins. Used with permission.

Although Figure 8-2 has all the columns completed, after completing step 5, we would only have the first column filled in. The remaining ones are described in steps 6, 7 and 8 that follow.

KPIs do not always need to be quantitative measures. Measurement data can come in all types. They can be text-based, as in yes or no for a discrete event, or they can be described as an estimated degree of completion (either as a % or even as basic as started, mid-way or complete). It is acceptable for scorecards to use subjective measures or measures scored with employee estimates rather than facts. These may be the most economical form of input data.

Figure 8-3 describes the differences between leading and lagging indicators. The simplest way to think of this is by asking and answering when is the actual score reported against the KPI, during the time period or at the end of the time period? (Of course, this begs the question for which time period, the past quarter, month, week, day or hour?) Figure 8-3 displays a two-dimensional view that is useful for understanding how leading and lagging KPIs relate to one another. The horizontal axis displays the time during the period, with the extreme right being the end. The vertical axis displays how deep a measure is and describes a root cause of the behaviour on the most upper-right measure, which I refer to as the benefiting KPI because this measure is a receiver of all the efforts of the actions reflected in the contributing KPIs.

Figure 8-3: Relating If-Then KPIs With Lead/Lag KPIs

A contributing KPI is a measure that is a deeper monitor of root causes. As the deep measures improve, their benefiting KPI eventually should too.

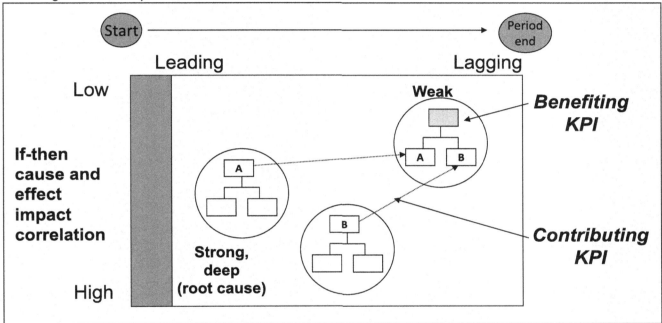

Source: Copyright Gary Cokins. Used with permission.

At this step in the enterprise performance management (EPM) process, the employee team will have selected the leading and lagging measures, configured among themselves and weighted in parallel to the levels of importance of the strategic objectives and corresponding action plans or business processes that they support. That is, with a properly cascaded scorecard hierarchy, strategic changes in strategy should result in new initiatives (or ones escalated in importance) and quickly be mirrored in the measurement system. At this point, and not before it, the scorecard as a mechanism is finally completed, but is not yet being used to measure and score actual data.

After this step, the correct KPI measures have been defined, weighted and related. The next step is inserting each KPI's target score (and their meter ranges) into the scorecard.

6. Select the target levels for each KPI for relevant time periods. Identify the performance deficiency gap.

With this step, we finally get to the point in which a specific measurement level or amount or a text description is agreed on. A target measurement level or amount should pass the test of 'if we were doing very well accomplishing the associated strategic objective, then this would be the level or amount of the specific measurement.'

7. Collect the actual KPIs, display the scores and compare to the targets.

This step is quite mechanical. Actual KPI measures are collected and inserted into the scorecard. The differences between the actual KPI score and its target KPI usually are calculated and displayed with a meter. Regardless of which side of the KPI meter the score differences lands, it is implicit that a favourable score positively contributes to accomplishing the strategic objectives that, when achieved, guides and excels the organisation toward realising its vision and mission.

Web-enabled scorecards, with traffic light colouring and alert messages as visual aids, add timely communications and discussion threads among managers and employees. That is, Web-enabled scorecards allow employees to actively write e-mails and record notes to investigate problems, focus on key needs and actively take corrective actions to improve their scores. These types of signals and alert messages that monitor real-time trends inform managers and employee teams that if something is likely to happen that will exceed a pain threshold, they will be notified before it happens.

8. Manage performance gaps to steer the organisation by interpreting and reacting to the score, then revising the actions plans.

If the strategy map and scorecard construction has been properly developed, what is now left is for good leadership to take over. At this point in the stage of maturity of using the scorecard, managers and employee teams are receiving continuous feedback on how they are performing. They also more clearly know what they are trying to attain—the strategic objectives that satisfy the vision and mission statements.

Unlike most internal e-mail messages, with scorecard feedback now Web-enabled for e-mail and discussion threads, the dialogues are intensely associated in the context of the strategy. A metaphor for a scorecard is like a crew team coxswain shouting to the crew. Here, the crew is having a dialogue among themselves, and the scorecard's measures (KPIs) have been selected in the context of the strategy. This ensures behaviour alignment. Context is important. It elevates this methodology well above traditional management by objectives methods and spreadsheet performance reports.

SCORECARDS AND STRATEGY MAPS: THE ENABLER FOR EPM

In today's environment, a business's road is no longer long and straight. It is windy, with bends and hills that don't allow much visibility or certainty about the future. Organisations must be agile and continuously transform their processes, cost structure and work activities. This is difficult to do when employees and managers do not understand their own strategies, the relevant performance measures, their cost structure and the economics of their environment. It is much easier for organisations to transform themselves when their performance measurement system links and communicates their strategies to the behaviour of their employees. Following are some reinforcing observations about scorecards:

- Scorecards help organisations move from being financially driven to mission-driven.
- If you fail to tie measures to strategy, you miss the chief benefit of the scorecard: alignment.
- The scorecard's purpose is to translate strategy into measures that uniquely communicate the senior executive's vision and mission to the organisation.
- Scorecard software systems, in which scorecards are routinely populated and published, promote e-mail dialogues for rapid messaging and note-taking documentation to prevent corporate amnesia that plagues organisations.

In short, failing to link measures to strategies will cause misalignment of the cost structure and priorities with the strategy. Because monitoring strategy attainment usually relies on output or results measures, lagging measures need to be translated into more process-operational leading measures reported during the period. Competing measures need to be minimised.

Unlike a trickle-down method of management, scorecarding is more of a trickle-up phenomenon. In order to produce good results, the expected performance measures should reflect solid, top-down planning, but the results—good or bad—will come from bottom-up performance. As an analogy, think of the organisation as a musical orchestra. You do not want to motivate all the musicians to play extremely loud. The balance comes from the correct decibels from each of the instruments.

If the measures selected are those that align employee behaviour to desired outcomes (eg, meeting strategic objectives), then the nearly-attained target measures will be met. Because the KPIs are derived from the strategy planning, the strategy itself is being achieved.

In summary, the need for reforms with organisational measures reflects the inability of senior management to communicate strategy changes and get their organisations to implement them in alignment with revised strategies.

EPM creates a shared vision that spans an organisation's value chain upstream and downstream with its suppliers and customers. An enterprise can effectively manage its strategic objectives and performance measurements in a way that maximises value to all stakeholders and constituents, not just individual operating groups. By focusing on one version of the truth, a scorecard system can optimise organisational efficiency, support continuous quality improvement and maximise the value of human and capital assets.

Scorecards provide a comprehensive tool that can coordinate and propel large numbers of employees. In the end, if the organisation is performing well, then the rewards go to the employees, the investors, in the form of financial returns, or to the governing boards of not-for-profit organisations in the form of mission accomplishment.

Are strategy maps and scorecards going to be a management fad? Management consultants who have transitioned into these services repeatedly say this methodology has a higher retention rate than the improvement programmes they have consulted on in the past. Strategy maps and scorecards make sense, address a true need and will likely be a keeper for organisations that experiment by trying new ideas.

Part 4

PLANNING, BUDGETING AND FORECASTING

'The three most important things you need in a business are customer satisfaction, employee morale, and cash flow. If you are growing customer satisfaction, your global market share is sure to grow. Employee satisfaction gets you productivity, quality, pride, and creativity. Cash flow is the pulse—the vital sign of life in a company.'
—Jack Welch, CEO (retired)
General Electric Inc.

9

PREDICTIVE ACCOUNTING AND BUDGETING WITH MARGINAL EXPENSE ANALYSIS[1]

Managers are increasingly shifting from reacting to after-the-fact outcomes to anticipating the future with predictive analysis and proactively making adjustments with better decisions. Despite some advances in the application of new costing techniques, are management accountants adequately satisfying the need for better cost planning information? Or is the gap widening?

There is a widening gap between what management accountants report and what managers and employee teams want. This does not mean that information produced by management accountants is of little value. In the last few decades, accountants have made significant strides in improving the utility and accuracy of the historical costs they calculate and report. The gap is caused by a shift in managers' needs, from just needing to know what things cost (such as a product cost) and why, to a need for reliable information about what their future costs will be and why.

Despite the accountants advancing a step to prioritise the increasing needs of managers, the managers have advanced two steps. In order to understand this widening gap and, more importantly, how accountants can narrow and ideally close the gap, let's review the broad landscape of accounting as described in Chapter 4, 'A Taxonomy of Accounting and Costing Methods.'

WHAT IS THE PURPOSE OF MANAGEMENT ACCOUNTING?

Contrary to beliefs that the only purpose of managerial accounting is to collect, transform and report data, its primary purpose is, first and foremost, to influence behaviour at all levels—from the desk of the CEO down to each employee—and it should do so by supporting decisions. A secondary purpose is to stimulate investigation and discovery by signalling relevant information (and consequently bringing focus) and generate questions.

The widening gap between what accountants report and what decision makers need involves the shift from analysing descriptive historical information to analysing predictive information, such as budgets and what-if scenarios. All decisions obviously can only affect the future because the past is already history. However much can be learned and leveraged from historical information. Although accountants are gradually improving the quality of reported history, decision makers are shifting their view toward better understanding the future.

This shift is a response to a more overarching shift in executive management styles, from a command and control emphasis that is reactive (such as scrutinising cost variance analysis of actual versus planned outcomes), to an anticipatory, proactive style in which organisational changes and adjustments, such as staffing levels, can be made before things happen and minor problems become big ones.

Figure 4-1 in Chapter 4 illustrated the large domain of accounting as a taxonomy with three components: tax accounting, financial accounting and managerial accounting. As a review, two types of data sources are displayed at the upper right in the figure. The upper source is from financial transactions and bookkeeping, such as purchases and payroll. The lower source is non-financial measures, such as payroll hours worked, retail items sold or gallons of liquid produced. These same measurements can be forecasted.

The financial accounting component in the figure is intended for external reporting, such as for regulatory agencies, banks, stockholders and the investment community. Financial accounting follows compliance rules aimed at economic valuation and, as such, is typically not adequate or sufficient for decision making, and the tax accounting component is its own world of legislated rules.

Our area of concern—the management accounting component—was segmented into three categories: cost accounting, the cost reporting and analysis and decision support with cost planning. To oversimplify a distinction between financial and managerial accounting, financial accounting is about valuation, and managerial accounting is about value creation through good decision making.

The message at the bottom of the figure is that the value, utility and usefulness of the information increases, arguably at an exponential rate, from the left side to the right side of the figure.

Figure 4-2 in Chapter 4 illustrated how a firm's view of its profit and expense structure changes as analysis shifts from the historical cost reporting view to a predictive cost planning view. The latter is the context from which decisions are considered and evaluated.

WHAT TYPES OF DECISIONS ARE MADE WITH MANAGERIAL ACCOUNTING INFORMATION?

University textbooks contain hundreds of pages on managerial and cost accounting. Let's try to distil all those pages into a few paragraphs. The broad decision-making categories for applying managerial accounting are as follows:

Rationalisation

Which products, stock keeping units, services, channels, routes, customers and so forth are best to retain or improve? Which are not and should potentially be abandoned or terminated?

Historical and descriptive costing (the left side of Figure 4-2) can be adequate to answer these questions. In part, this explains the growing popularity in applying activity-based cost principles to supplement traditional direct costing. Considerable diversity and variation exists in routes, channels, customers and so forth that cause a relative increase in an organisation's indirect and shared expenses to manage the resulting complexity. IT expenses are a growing one. Having the direct and indirect costs become a relevant starting point allows you to know what the variations cost. This answers the 'What?' question discussed in Chapter 4. It is difficult, arguably impossible, to answer the subsequent 'So what?' question without having the facts. Otherwise, conclusions are based on gut feeling, intuition, misleading information or politics.

Planning and Budgeting

Based on forecasts of future demand volume and mix for types of services or products, combined with assumptions of other proposed changes, how much will it cost to match demand with supplied resources (eg, workforce staffing levels)?

When questions like these and many more like them are asked, one needs more than a crystal ball to answer them. This is where the predictive view of costing (the right side of Figure 4-2) fits in, and the predictive view arguably is the sweet spot of costing. On an annual cycle, this is the budgeting process. However, executives are increasingly demanding rolling financial forecasts at shorter intervals, partially due to the fact that the annual budget can quickly become obsolete, and future period assumptions, especially continuously revised sales forecasts, become more certain. At its core, this costing sweet spot is about resource capacity planning (the ability to convert and reflect physical operational events into the language of money) expenses and costs.

Capital Expense Justification

Is the return on investment of a proposed asset purchase, such as equipment or an information system, justified?

If we purchase equipment, technology or a system, will the financial benefits justify the investment? A question like this involves what microeconomics refers to as *capital budgeting*. Capital budgeting analysis typically involves comparing a baseline, reflecting business as usual, with an alternative scenario that includes spending on (ie, investing in) an asset in which the expected benefits will continue well beyond a year's duration. An example would be investing in an automated warehouse to replace manual, pick-and-pack labour. Some refer to the associated investment justification analysis as *same as, except for* or comparing the as-is state with the to-be state. A distinction of capital budgeting is that it involves discounted cash flow (DCF) equations. DCF equations reflect the net present value of money, incorporating the time that it would take for that same money to earn income at some rate if it were applied elsewhere (eg, a bank certificate of deposit).The rate is often called the organisation's cost of capital.

Make Versus Buy, and General Outsourcing Decisions

Should we continue to do work ourselves or contract with a third party?

If we choose to have a third party make our product or deliver our service—basically outsourcing (or vice versa by bringing a supplier's work in-house)—then how much of our expenses remain, and how much will we remove (or add)? This type of decision is similar to the logic and math of capital budgeting. The same description of the capital budgeting method applies, measuring 'same as, except for' incremental changes. Activity-based costing techniques ideally should be applied because the primary variable is the work activities that the third party contractor will now perform, which replace the current in-house work. Because cost is not the only variable that shifts, a service-level agreement with the contactor should be a standard practice.

Process and Productivity Improvement

What can be changed? How do you identify opportunities? How do you compare and differentiate high impact opportunities from nominal ones?

Some organisation's operations functions focus on reducing costs and future cost avoidance. (Strategic profitable revenue enhancement is addressed with managerial accounting for rationalisation.) These operational functions are tasked with productivity improvement challenges, and they are less interested in understanding strategic profitability analysis, that is, which of our priced products and services makes or loses money, and more on streamlining processes, reducing waste and low value-added work activities and increasing asset utilisation. This is the area of Six Sigma quality initiatives, lean management principles and just-in-time scheduling techniques. Examples of these types of costs are as follows:

- Unit costs of outputs and benchmarking
- Target costing
- Cost of quality
- Value-adding attributes (such as non-value added vs. value-added).
- Resource consumption accounting (RCA)
- German cost accounting (*Grenzplankostenrechnung* [GPK])
- Accounting for a lean management environment (also Kaizen costing)
- Theory of constraint's throughput accounting

The term *cost estimating* is a general one. It applies in all the preceding decision-making categories. One might conclude that the first category, rationalisation, focuses only on historical costs and, thus, does not require cost estimates. However, the impact on resource expenses from adding or dropping various work-consuming outputs (ie, products, services and customers) also require cost estimates to validate the merit of a proposed rationalisation decision.

Activity-Based Cost Management as a Foundation for Predictive Accounting

In the late 1990s, the more mature and advanced activity-based costing users increasingly began using their activity-based cost management (ABC/M) calculated unit cost rates for intermediate work outputs and for products and services as a basis for estimating costs. As previously described, popular uses for the activity-based costing data for cost estimating have been to calculate customer order quotations, perform make versus buy analysis, and budget. The ABC/M data were being recognised as a predictive planning tool. It is now apparent that the data have a tremendous amount of utility for both examining the as-is current condition of the organisation and achieving a desired to-be state. (As mentioned earlier, a more robust version of ABC/M is RCA, which is based on the German accounting practice GPK for marginal expense analysis and flexible budgeting for operational control. RCA is a comprehensive approach that focuses on resources and capacity management logic with ABC/M principles.[2])

Cost estimating is often referred to as *what-if scenarios*. Regardless of what the process is called, we are talking about decisions being made about the future, and managers wanting to evaluate the consequences of those decisions. In these situations, the future of the organisation is not very distant and, in some way, the quantity and mix of activity drivers will be placing demands on the work that the organisation will need to do. The resources required to do the work are the expenses. Assumptions are made about the outputs that are expected. Assumptions should also be made about the intermediate outputs and the labyrinth of inter-organisational relationships that will be called upon to generate the expected final outcomes.

MAJOR CLUE: CAPACITY ONLY EXISTS AS A RESOURCE

As most organisations plan for their next month, quarter or year, the level of resources supplied is routinely re-planned to roughly match the firm customer orders and expected future order demands. In reality, the level of planned resources must always exceed customer demand to allow for some protective buffer, surge and sprint capacity. This also helps improve customer service in shipping performance. However management accountants will be constantly disturbed if they cannot answer the question, 'How much unused and spare capacity do I have?' because in their minds, this excess capacity equates to non-value-added costs.

The broad topic of unused and idle capacity will likely be a thorny issue for absorption costing. As management accountants better understand operations, they will be constantly improving their ability to segment and isolate the unused capacity (and the nature of its cost) by individual resource. Managerial accountants will be increasingly able to measure unused capacity either empirically or by deductive logic based on projected standard cost rates. Furthermore, accountants will be able to segment and assign this unused capacity expense to various processes, owners, the sales function or senior management. This will eliminate over-charging (and over-stating) product costs resulting from including unused capacity costs that the product did not cause.

Figure 9-1 illustrates that the effort level to adjust capacity becomes easier farther out in time. It takes a while to convert in-case resources into as-needed ones. However committed expenses (in-case) today can be more easily converted into contractual (as-needed) arrangements in a shorter time period than was possible ten years ago. Fixed expenses can become variable expenses. The rapid growth in the temporary staffing industry is evidence. Organisations are replacing full-time employees who are paid regardless of the demand level with contractors who are staffed and paid at the demand level, which may be measured in hours.

Figure 9-1: Capacity Only Exists as Resources

In the very short term, you would not fire employees on Tuesday due to low work load, then hire them back on Wednesday. In the future you may replace full-time employees with contractors, or lease assets you might have purchased. In this way, so-called 'fixed costs' behave variably.

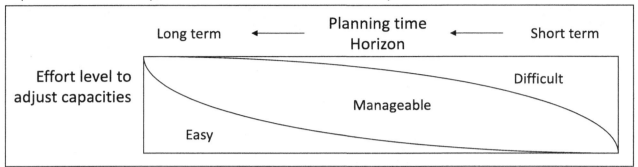

Source: Copyright Gary Cokins. Used with permission.

Understanding the cost of the resource workload used to make a product or deliver a service is relevant to making these resource re-allocation decisions. Ignoring incremental changes in the actual resources (ie, expense spending) when making decisions can eventually lead to a cost structure that may become inefficient and ineffective for the organisation. There will always be a need to adjust the capacity based on changes in future demand volume and mix. This, in turn, equates to raising or lowering specific expenses on resources.

PREDICTIVE ACCOUNTING INVOLVES MARGINAL EXPENSE CALCULATIONS

In forecasting, the demand volume and mix of the outputs are estimated, and the unknown level of resource expenditures that will be required to produce and deliver the volume and mix is solved for. You basically are determining the capacity requirements of the resources. Estimating future levels of resource expense cash outflows becomes complex because resources come in discrete, discontinuous amounts. For example, you cannot hire one-third of an employee. That is, resource expenses do not immediately vary with each incremental increase or decrease in end-unit volume. Traditional accountants address this with what they refer to as a *step-fixed* category of expenses.

The predictive accounting method involves extrapolations that use baseline physical and cost consumption rates that are calibrated from prior period ABC/M calculations. Managerial accountants relate predictive accounting to a form of flexible budgeting (which is normally applied annually to a 12-month time span).

Figure 9-2 illustrates how capacity planning is the key to the solution. Planners and budgeters initially focus on the direct and recurring resource expenses, not the indirect and overhead support expenses. They almost always begin with estimates of future demand in terms of volumes and mix. Then, by relying on standards and averages (such as the product routings and bills-of material used in manufacturing systems), planners and budgeters calculate the future required levels of manpower and spending. The predictive accounting method suggests that this same approach can be applied to the indirect and overhead areas as well or to processes where the organisation often has a wrong impression that they have no tangible outputs.

Figure 9-2: Predictive Accounting Information Flow

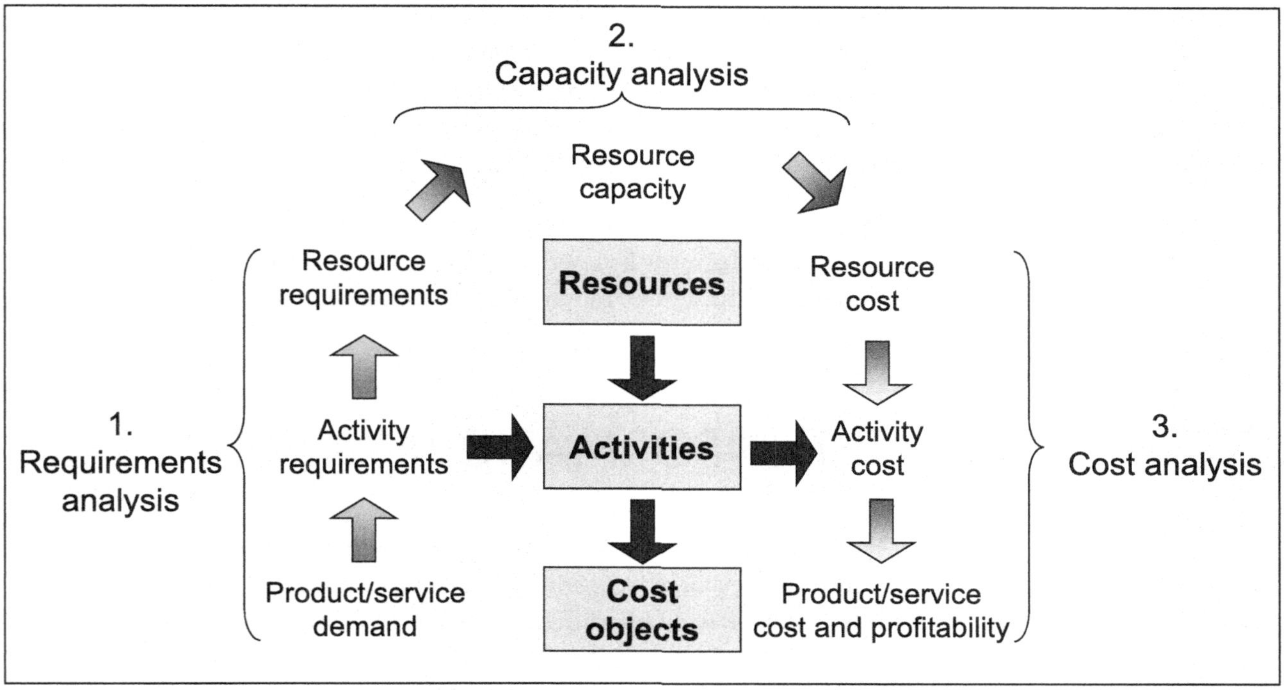

Source: Copyright Gary Cokins. Used with permission.

Demand volume drives activity and resource requirements. Predictive accounting is forward-focused, but it uses actual historical performance data to develop baseline consumption rates. Activity-based planning and budgeting assesses the quantities of workload demands that are ultimately placed on resources. In step 1 in Figure 9-2, predictive accounting first asks, 'How much activity workload is required for each output of cost object?' These are the work activity requirements. Then predictive accounting asks, 'How many resources are needed to meet that activity workload?' In other words, a workload can be measured as the number of units of an activity requires to produce a quantity of cost objects.

The determination of expense does not occur until after the activity volume has been translated into resource capacity using the physical resource driver rates from the direct costing and ABC/M model. These rates are regularly expressed in hours, full-time equivalents, square feet, pounds, gallons and so forth.

As a result of step 1, there will be a difference between the existing resources available and the resources that will be required to satisfy the plan—the resource requirements. That is, at this stage, organisations usually discover they may have too much of what they do not need and not enough of what they do need to meet the customers' expected service levels (eg, to deliver on time). The consequence of having too much implies a cost of unused capacity. The consequence of having too little is a limiting constraint that, if not addressed, implies there will be a decline in customer service levels.

In step 2, a reasonable balance must be achieved between the operational and financial measures. Now capacity must be analysed. One option is for the budgeters, planners or management accountants to evaluate how much to adjust the shortage and excess of actual resources to respond to the future demand load. Senior management may or may not allow the changes. A maximum expense impact exists that near-term financial targets (and executive compensation plan bonuses) will tolerate. These capacity adjustments represent real resources with real changes in cash outlay expenses, if they were to be enacted.

Assume that management agrees to the new level of resources without further analysis or debate. In step 3 of the flow in Figure 9-2, the new level of resource expenditures can be determined and then translated into the expenses of the work centres and, eventually, into the costs of the products, service lines, channels and customers. Step 3 is classic cost accounting—but for a future period. Some call this a *pro forma* calculation. The quantities of the projected resource and activity drivers are applied, and new budgeted or planned costs can be calculated for products, service lines, outputs, customers and service recipients.

At this point, however, the financial impact may not be acceptable. It may show too small a financial return. When the financial result is unacceptable, management has options other than to continue to keep re-adjusting resource capacity levels. For example, they can limit the amount of customer orders they accept. These other options may not have much effect on expenses.

DECOMPOSING THE INFORMATION FLOWS FIGURE

Figure 9-3 decomposes Figure 9-2. It reveals five types of adjustments that planners and budgeters can consider to align their expected demand with resource expenditures to achieve desired financial results. This approach has been called a 'closed loop activity-based planning and budgeting' framework.

Figure 9-3: Resource Capacity Planning and Costing

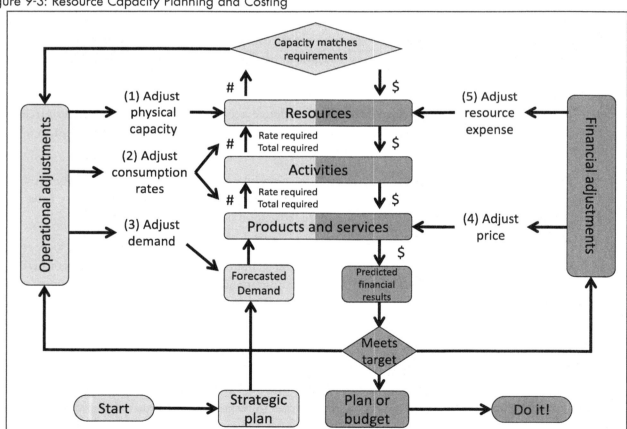

Source: Adapted from cam-i.org/docs/Methods_and_Applications.pdf.

Each of the five numbered options is intended to improve results, however, the relative impact of each adjustment will be unique to each organisation and its situation. As previously described, the predictive accounting model uses the forecasted demand quantities as its source input to determine if there is a degree of imbalance between the required and current existing resources.

Assuming that the result will be shortages and excesses of capacity, management can physically do the following:

- **Adjust capacity.** Additional manpower, supplies, overtime, equipment and the like can be purchased for shortages. There can be scale-backs and removals of people and machines for excesses.

- **Adjust consumption rates.** If possible, the speed and efficiency of the existing resources can be cranked up or down. If, for example, the increase in manpower makes a decision wasteful, fewer people can be hired, with an assumed productivity rate increase assumed.

- **Adjust demand.** If resources remain constrained, demand can be governed or rationed.

The latter two options are operational but also affect the level of resource expenses required. After this cycle of adjustments balances capacity of supply with demand, if the financial results are still unsatisfactory, management can make two incremental financial changes:

- **Adjust pricing.** In commercial for-profit enterprises or full cost recovery operations, pricing can be raised or lowered. This directly affects the 'top line' revenues. Of course, care is required because the price elasticity could cause changes in volume that more than offset the price changes.

- **Adjust resource cost.** If possible, wage levels or purchase prices of materials can be re-negotiated.

Predictive accounting acknowledges that there is a substantial amount of expenses that do not vary with a unit volume of final output. These expenses are not variable costs as determined by an incremental new expense for each incremental unit of output. As mentioned, resources often come in discontinuous amounts. Economists refer to these as *step-fixed costs*. An organisation cannot purchase one-third of a machine or hire half of an employee. Predictive accounting recognises the step-fixed costs in step 2, where resource capacity is adjusted. It recognises that as external unit volumes fluctuate, then

- some workload costs do eventually vary based on a batch-size of output or on some other discretionary factor.

- some resource expenditures will be acquired or retired as a whole and indivisible resource, thus, creating step-fixed expenses (ie, adding or removing used and unused capacity expenses).

Absorption costing is descriptive, and the only economic property for costing you need to deal with is traceability of cost objects back to the resources they consume. However, the descriptive ABC/M data is used for predictive purposes. The data provide inferences. In contrast, predictive accounting is forward-looking. Predictive accounting strives to monitor the impact of decisions or plans in terms of the external cash funds flow of an organisation. In the predictive view, determining the level of resource expenses gets trickier because you now have to consider an additional economic property—variability. The variability of resources is affected by two factors: (1) the step-fixed function because resources come in discontinuous amounts, and (2) adjustability of resources because the time delay to add or remove resource capacity can range from short to long.

Financial analysts simplistically classify costs as being either fixed or variable within the so-called 'relevant range' of volume. In reality, the classification of expenses as sunk, fixed, semi-fixed, semi-variable or variable depends on the decision being made. In the short term, many expenses will not and cannot be changed. In the long-term, many of the expenses (ie, capacity) can be adjusted.

FRAMEWORK TO COMPARE AND CONTRAST EXPENSE ESTIMATING METHODS

Figure 9-4 presents a framework that describes various methods of predictive cost estimating. The horizontal axis is the planning time horizon, short term to long term, right to left. The vertical axis describes the types and magnitudes of change in demands of the future relative to the recent past.

Figure 9-4: Methods of Forecasting Results

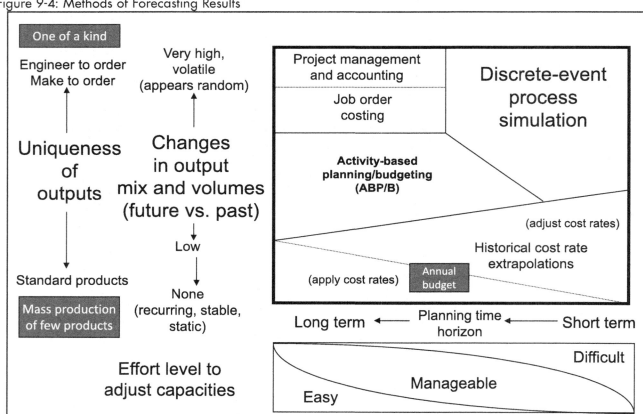

Source: Copyright Gary Cokins. Used with permission.

Examine the lower part of the figure, which illustrates the level of effort to adjust capacity across the planning time horizon. It describes expenses as becoming more variable and less committed as the planning time horizon lengthens. Historical cost rates can be more easily applied for longer time frame decisions, and there are fewer step-fixed expense issues. No defined boundary lines exist between the various zones, and there is overlap as one estimating method gives way to another as being superior.

Figure 9-4 illustrates in the upper right corner that as the time period to adjust capacity shortens and simultaneously the number of changes in conditions from the past substantially increase, it becomes risky to rely exclusively on rate-based extrapolation methods for cost forecasting. Discrete event simulation tools may provide superior and more reliable answers in this zone relative to the other methods. It can evaluate and validate decisions in any zone but, in particular, the upper right corner of Figure 9-4.

PREDICTIVE COSTING IS MODELLING

A commercial organisation ultimately manages itself by understanding where it makes and loses money or whether the impact of a decision produces incremental revenues superior to incremental expenses. Organisations are increasingly achieving a much better understanding of their contribution profit margins using ABC/M data. By leveraging ABC/M with predictive accounting and discrete event process simulation tools, an organisation can produce a fully integrated plan, including budgets and rolling financial forecasts. It can be assured that its plan is more feasible, determine the level of resources and expenditures to implement that plan, then view and compare the projected results of that plan against its current performance to manage its various profit margins.

The combination of these tools allows boardroom-level thinking to begin with the company's complete income statement, generate a feasible operating plan and restate the results of that plan with an income statement—again, for boardroom reporting. Advocates of simulation planning software believe that the computing power of personal computers or seamless integration with servers, or both, now adequately provides simulation information that is comprehensive, finite-scheduled and rule-based and allows for various assumptions about uncertainty. Others argue that this is a last resort and that good modelling provides sufficiently accurate results.

All of this may sound like material from an introductory Economics textbook. In some ways it is, but there is a difference. In the textbooks, marginal expense analysis was something easily described but extremely difficult to compute due to all the complexities and interdependencies of resources and their costs. In the past, computing technology was the impediment. Now things have reversed. Technology is no longer the impediment—the thinking is. How you configure the predictive accounting model and what assumptions you make becomes critical to calculating the appropriate required expenses and their pro forma calculated costs.

DEBATES ABOUT COSTING METHODS

Confusion can arise because some of the costing methods calculate and report different costs that are not just variations in cost accuracy but are also different cost amounts. For example, should there be two or more different, co-existing cost reporting methods that report dissimilar numbers? One tactical costing method might be used for operations and making short-term decisions, whereas another strategic costing method (for planning, marketing, pricing and sales analysts to evaluate profit margins) is used for longer-term decisions.

There will be debates, but, eventually, some form of consensus will triumph within an organisation. The underlying arguments may be due to the inappropriate usage of standard costing information—and the potential inappropriate actions that may result. Therefore, key factor for deciding which costing method to use should be how does it handle economic projections? Can it accommodate classifying resource expenses as variable, semi-variable, fixed, sunk or as unavoidable or avoidable (ie, allowing for capacity adjustment decisions)? Does it isolate unused or idle capacity expenses?

The good news is that organisations are challenging traditional accounting. So in the end, any accounting treatments that yield better decision making should prevail. The co-existence of two or more costing approaches may cause confusion over which one reports the correct cost, but that is a different problem. What matters is that organisations are seeking better ways to apply managerial accounting techniques to make better decisions.

Endnotes

1 The ideas in this chapter on activity-based resource planning are based on research from a professional society. The researchers are from the Activity Based Budgeting Project Team of the Consortium of Advanced—International (CAM-I) Cost Management Systems (CMS) group. More information can be found at www.cam-i.org.

2 You can learn more about resource consumption accounting at www.rcainfo.com.

10

WHAT'S BROKEN ABOUT BUDGETING?

How many people in your organisation love the annual budgeting process? Probably none. The mere mention of the word *budget* raises eyebrows and evokes cynicism. As a simple test, how many options in Box 10-1 would be checked off as applicable to your organisation? If you check all, you are not alone.

Box 10-1: A Quiz. 'Our budgeting exercise...'

☐ is invasive and time-consuming ... with few benefits.

☐ takes 14 months from start to end.

☐ requires two or more executive 'tweaks' at the end.

☐ is obsolete in two months due to events and re-organisations.

☐ starves the departments with truly valid needs.

☐ caves in to the 'loudest voice' and 'political muscle.'

☐ rewards veteran sand-baggers who are experts at padding.

☐ incorporates last year's inefficiencies into this year's budget.

☐ is over-stated from the prior year's 'use-it-or-lose-it' spending.

Source: Copyright Gary Cokins. Used with permission.

What is broken about the annual budgeting process? We will more deeply discuss some of the following issues related to budgeting:

- *Obsolete budgeting.* The budget data is obsolete within weeks after it is published because of ongoing changes in the environment. Customers and competitors usually change their behaviour after the budget is published, and a prudent reaction to these changes often cannot be accommodated in the budget. In addition, today's budget process takes an extraordinarily long time, sometimes exceeding a year, during which the organisation often re-shuffles and resizes.

- *Bean-counter budgeting.* The budget is considered a fiscal exercise produced by the accountants and is disconnected from the strategy of the executive team—and from the mission-critical spending needed to implement the strategy.

- *Political budgeting.* The loudest voice, the greatest political muscle and the prior year's budget levels should not be valid ways to award resources for next year's spending.

- *Over-scrutinised budgeting.* Often the budget is revised mid-year or, more frequently, with new forecast spending. Then, an excess amount of attention focuses on analysing the differences between the actual and projected expenses. These include budget-to-forecast, last-forecast-to-current-forecast, actual-to-budget, actual-to-forecast and so forth. This reporting provides lifetime job security for the budget analysts in the accounting department.

- *Sandbagging budgeting.* The budget numbers that come from lower- and mid-level managers often mislead senior executives because of sandbagging (ie, padding) by the veteran managers who know how to play the game.

- *Wasteful budgeting.* Budgets do not identify waste. In fact, inefficiencies in the current business processes are often 'baked into' next year's budget. Budgets do not support continuous improvement.

- *Blow-it-all budgeting.* Reckless use-it-or-lose-it spending is standard practice for managers during the last fiscal quarter. Budgets can be an invitation to managers to spend needlessly.

The annual budget is steeped in tradition, yet the effort of producing it heavily outweighs the benefits it supposedly yields. How can budgeting be reformed? Or should the budget process be abandoned altogether because its inflexible, fixed, social contract incentives to managers drives behaviour counter to the organisation's changing goals and its unwritten earnings contract with shareholders? If the budget is abandoned, then what should replace its underlying purpose?

THE EVOLUTIONARY HISTORY OF BUDGETS

Why were budgets invented? Organisations seem to go through an irreversible life cycle that leads them toward specialisation and, eventually, to turf protection. When organisations are originally created, managing spending is fairly straightforward. With the passing of time, the number and variety of their products and service lines change, as do the needs of their customers. This introduces complexity and results in more indirect expenses and overhead to manage the newly created complexity.

Following an organisation's initial creation, all the workers are reasonably focused on fulfilling the needs of whatever created the organisation in the first place. Despite early attempts to maintain flexibility, organisations slowly evolve into separate functions. As the functions create their own identities and staff, they seem to become fortresses. In many of them, the work becomes the jealously guarded property of the occupants. Inside each fortress, allegiances grow, and people speak their own languages—an effective way to spot intruders and confuse communications.

As more time passes, organisations become internally hierarchical. This structure exists even though the transactions and workflows that provide value and service to the customers pass through and across internal and artificial organisational boundaries. These now-accepted management hierarchies are often referred to within the organisation itself, as well as in management literature, as *silos, stovepipes* or *smokestacks*. The structure causes managers to act in a self-serving way, placing their functional needs above those of the cross-functional processes to which each function contributes. In effect, the managers place their personal needs above the needs of their co-workers and customers.

At this stage in its life, the organisation becomes less sensitive to the sources of demand placed on it from the outside and changes in customer needs. In other words, the organisation begins to lose sight of its raison d'être. The functional silos compete for resources and blame one another for any of the organisation's inexplicable and continuing failures to meet the needs of its customers. Arguments emerge about the source of the organisation's inefficiencies, but they are difficult to explain.

The accountants do not help matters. They equate the functional silos to the responsibility cost centre view that they capture expense transactions in their general ledger accounting system. When they request each cost centre manager to submit the next year's budget, it ultimately is an increment or decrement game, that is, each manager begins with their best estimate of their current year's expected total spending—line item by line item—and they incrementally increase it with a percentage. Budgeting software reinforces this bad habit by making it easy to make these calculations. At the very extreme, next year's spending for each line is computed as shown in Figure 10-1. Using spreadsheet software, you multiply the first line item expense by the increment, in this example, by 5%, and simply copy and paste that formula for every line item below it. This is what leads to the use-it-or-lose-it, unnecessary, blow-it-all spending earlier described.

Figure 10-1: Spreadsheet Budgeting—It Is Incremental

	a	b	c
1		Current Year	Budget Year
2	Wages	$ 400,000.00	Formula = Column B * 1.05
3	Supplies	$ 50,000.00	
4	Rent	$ 20,000.00	Copy down
5	Computer	$ 40,000.00	
6	Travel	$ 30,000.00	
7	Phone	$ 20,000.00	
8	Total	$ 560,000.00	

Sheet 1

Source: Copyright Gary Cokins. Used with permission.

By this evolution point in budgeting, there is poor end-to-end visibility about what exactly drives what inside the organisation. Some organisations eventually evolve into intransigent bureaucracies. Some functions become so embedded inside the broader organisation that their work level is insensitive to changes in the number and types of external requests. Fulfilling these requests was the reason why their function was created in the first place. They become insulated from the outside world. This is not a pleasant story, but it is pervasive.

A SEA CHANGE IN ACCOUNTING AND FINANCE

How can budgeting be reformed? Let's step back and ask broader questions. What are the impacts of the changing role of the CFO? How many times have you seen the obligatory diagram with the organisation shown in a central circle and a dozen inward-pointing arrows representing the menacing forces and pressures the organisation faces, such as outsourcing, globalisation, governance, brand preservation and so forth? Well, it's all true and real. If the CFO's function is evolving from a bean counter and reporter of history into a strategic business adviser and an enterprise risk and regulatory compliance manager, what are CFOs doing about the archaic budget process?

Progressive CFOs now view budgeting as consisting of three streams of spending that converge into one:

- *Recurring expenses.* Budgeting becomes an ongoing resource capacity planning exercise, similar to a 1970s factory manager who must project the operation's manpower planning and material purchasing requirements.

- *Non-recurring expenses.* The budget includes one-time investments or project cash outlays to implement strategic initiatives.

- *Discretionary expenses.* The budget includes optional spending that is non-strategic.

Of the broad portfolio of interdependent methodologies that make up today's enterprise performance management (EPM) framework, two methods deliver the capability to accurately project the recurring and non-recurring spending streams:

1. *Activity-based planning.* In the 1990s, activity-based costing (ABC) solved the structural deficiencies of myopic general ledger cost-centre reporting for calculating accurate costs of outputs (such as products, channels and customers). The general ledger does not recognise cross-functional business processes that deliver the results, and its broad cost allocations of the now substantial indirect expenses introduce grotesque cost distortions. ABC corrects those deficiencies. Advances to ABC's historical snapshot view transformed it into activity-based management (ABM). These advances project forecasts of customer demand item volume and mix and forecast the elusive customer cost-to-serve requirements. In effect, ABC is calculated backward and named activity-based planning, based on ABC's calibrated consumption rates to determine the needed capacity and, thus, the needed recurring expenses. Without that spending, service levels will deteriorate.

2. *The balanced scorecard and strategy maps.* By communicating the executive strategy and involving managers and employee teams to identify the projects and initiatives required to achieve the strategy map's objectives, non-recurring expenses are funded. Without that spending, managers will be unjustly flagged as failing to achieve the key performance indicators they are responsible for in their balanced scorecards.

THE FINANCIAL MANAGEMENT INTEGRATED INFORMATION DELIVERY PORTAL

Today's solution to solve the budgeting conundrum and the organisation's backward-looking focus is to begin with a single, integrated data platform—popularly called a *business intelligence* platform—and its Web-based reporting and analysis capabilities. Speed to knowledge is now a competitive differentiator.

The emphasis for improving an organisation and driving higher value must shift from stringent controlling to automated, forward-looking planning. With a common platform replacing disparate data sources, enhanced with input data integrity cleansing features and data mining capabilities, an organisation can create a flexible and collaborative planning environment. It can provide on-demand information access to all for what-if scenarios and trade-off analysis. For the bold CFO, who is not wary of radical change, continuous and valid rolling financial forecasts can replace the rigid annual budget. Organisations need to be able to answer more questions than just 'Are we going to hit our numbers in December?' That's not planning but, rather, performance evaluation. For the traditional CFO, the integrated data platform offers a sorely needed high speed budgeting process.

In addition, statistical forecasting can be combined with the integrated information on the platform, resulting in customer demand forecasting that seamlessly links to operational systems, activity-based planning and balanced scorecard initiatives for the ultimate financial view that the CFO can now offer to his or her managers. Real time or right time feedback to managers is part of the package.

All of this—traffic light dashboards, profitability reporting and analysis, consolidation reporting, dynamic drill-down, customisable exception alert messaging to minimise surprises, Excel linkages, multiple versioning and more—is available for decision making on a single shared solution architecture platform. EPM resolves major problems, including lack of visibility to causality, lack of timely and reliable information, poor understanding of the executive team's strategy and wasted resources due to misaligned work processes.

Some organisations have become sufficiently frustrated with the annual budgeting process that they have abandoned creating a budget. An international research and membership collaborative called the Beyond Budgeting Round Table (BBRT)[1] advocates that rather than attempting to tightly control spending on a line-by-line basis, it is better to step back and question what the purposes of budgeting are. Their conclusion is that organisations would be better off moving away from long-term financial projections at a detailed level and replacing this form of monitoring by empowering managers with more freedom to make local spending decisions, including hiring employees. BBRT believes in removing second-guess approvals from higher level managers and granting managers more decision rights. BBRT views fiscal year-end budget figures as if they are a fixed contract that managers will strive for rather than react to unassumed changes when the budget was created. In place of budget spending variance controls, BBRT advocates a shift in reporting emphasis and also accountability with consequences on outcomes (performance reporting) not on the inputs. BBRT believes that secondary purposes for budgeting, such as cash flow projections for the treasury function, can be attained with modelling techniques performed by analysts.

Regardless of how an organisation approaches its own reforms to budgeting, EPM provides confidence in the numbers, which improves trust among managers. What will currently accelerate the adoption of reforms to the budgeting process and an EPM culture—senior management's attitude and willpower or the information technology that can realise the vision described here? I would choose both.

Endnotes

1 For more information, go to www.bbrt.org.

11

PUT YOUR MONEY WHERE YOUR STRATEGY IS

Two easy ways for executive teams to attempt to raise profits is to lay off employees to cut costs or to lower prices to take away market share from their competitors. However these merely are short-term fixes. An organisation cannot endlessly reduce its costs and prices to achieve long-term sustained prosperity.

Entrepreneurs know the age-old adage 'you need to spend money to make money.' However, reigning in an organisation's spending can be haphazard. Rather than evaluating where the company can cut costs, it is more prudent to ask where and how the organisation should spend money to increase long-term sustained value. This involves budgeting for future expenses, but the budgeting process has deficiencies.

A BUDGETING PROBLEM

Companies cannot succeed by standing still. If you are not continuously improving, then others will soon catch up. This is one reason why Professor Michael E. Porter, author of the seminal 1970 book on competitive edge strategies, *Competitive Strategy: Techniques for Analyzing Industries and Competitors*, asserted that an important strategic approach is continuous differentiation of products and services to enable premium pricing. However some organisations so firmly believed in their past successes that they went bankrupt because they had become risk-adverse to changing what they perceived to be effective strategies.

Strategy implementation is considered one of the major failures of executive teams. At a recent conference Dr David Norton, co-author with Professor Robert S. Kaplan of *The Balanced Scorecard: Translating Strategy into Action* referenced in Part 3, Chapter 7, 'The Promise and Perils of the Balanced Scorecard,' reported 'Nine out of 10 organizations fail to successfully implement their strategy. ... The problem is not that organizations don't manage their strategy well; it is they do not formally manage their strategy.'[1] Empirical evidence confirms that companies poorly implement strategy. Involuntary replacement of North American CEOs in 2006 will beat the record high set just the previous year.[2] In defence of executives, they often formulate good strategies—their problem is failure to implement them.

One of the obstacles preventing successful strategy achievement is the annual budgeting process. In the worst situations, the budgeting process is limited to a fiscal exercise administered by the accountants, who are typically disconnected from the executive team's strategic intentions. A less difficult situation, but still not a solution, is one in which the accountants do consider the executive team's strategic objectives, but the initiatives required to achieve the strategy are not adequately funded in the budget. Remember, you have to spend money to make money.

In addition, the budgeting process tends to be insensitive to changes in future volumes and mix of forecast products and services. As described in the prior chapter, the next year's budgeted spending is typically incremented or decreased by a few percentage points for each cost centre from the prior year's spending.

Components of the enterprise performance management (EPM) framework can be drawn on to resolve these limitations. In Figure 11-1, the large arrow at the right illustrates that the correct and valid amount of spending for capacity and consumed expenses should be derived from two broad workload streams that cause the need for spending—demand-driven and project-driven workload streams. Demand-driven expenses are operational and recur daily. In contrast, project-driven spending is non-recurring and can be from days to years in time duration.

Figure 11-1: Resource Requirements Are Derived

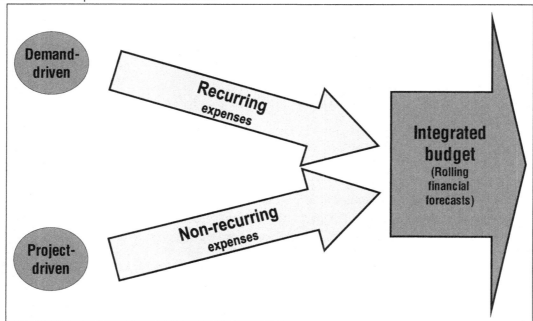

Source: Copyright Gary Cokins. Used with permission.

VALUE IS CREATED FROM PROJECTS AND INITIATIVES, NOT STRATEGIC OBJECTIVES

A popular solution for failed strategy implementation is the evolving methodology of a strategy map with its companion, the balanced scorecard. Their combined purpose is to link operations to strategy. By using these methodologies, alignment of employees' work and priorities can be attained without any disruption from re-structuring the organisational chart. The balanced scorecard directly connects the executive team's strategy to individuals, regardless of their departments or matrix-management arrangements.

Although many organisations claim to use dashboards and scorecards, there is little consensus on how to design or apply these tools. At best, the balanced scorecard has achieved a brand status but without prescribed rules on how to construct or use it. For example, many companies claim to have a balanced scorecard, but it may have been developed in the absence of a strategy map from executives.

The strategy map arguably is many orders of magnitude more important than the balanced scorecard. Therefore, when organisations simply display their so-called scorecard of actual versus planned or targeted measurements on a dashboard, how do the users know that the key performance indicators (KPIs) displayed in the dials reflect the strategic intent of their executives? They may not. At a basic level, the balanced scorecard simply is a feedback mechanism to inform users how they are performing on pre-selected measures that are ideally causally linked. To improve, much more information than just reporting your score is needed.

One source of confusion in the strategy management process involves misunderstandings of the role of projects and initiatives. For the minority of companies that realise the importance of first developing their strategy map before jumping ahead to designing their balanced scorecards, there is another methodology challenge. Should organisations first select and set the targets for the scorecard KPIs, then subsequently determine the specific projects and initiatives that will help reach those targets? Or should the sequence be reversed? Should organisations first propose the projects and initiatives based on the strategy map's various theme objectives, and then derive the KPIs with their target measures after?

We could debate the proper order. In Part 3 I argued that projects and initiatives should be defined from the strategy map. Putting this argument aside, what matters more is that the projects and initiatives are financially funded regardless of how they are identified. Figure 11-2 revisits Figure 7-2, described in Chapter 7, on implementing strategy maps and the balanced scorecard.

Figure 11-2: (1) Non-Recurring Expenses/Strategic Initiatives

Budgeting is typically disconnected from the strategy. This problem is solved if management funds the managers' projects.

Measurement period	1st quarter					
	Strategic objective	Identify projects, initiatives or processes	KPI measure	KPI target	KPI actual	Comments/ explanation
Executive team	X			X		
Managers and employees		X	X		*Their score*	X
					<----- *Period results* ------->	

Source: Copyright Gary Cokins. Used with permission.

Regarding the second column of 'x' choices in Figure 11-2, what if the managers and employee teams that identified the projects are not granted spending approval by the executives for those initiatives? Assuming that KPIs with targets were established for those projects, these managers will poorly and unfavourably score. Worse yet, the strategic objectives the projects are intended to achieve will not be accomplished. By isolating this spending as strategy expenses, the organisation protects them—otherwise it is like destroying the seeds for future success and growth. Capital budgeting is a more mature practice and not as much of an issue as budgeting for strategic projects and initiatives.

Value creation does not directly come from defining mission, vision and strategy maps. It is the alignment of employees' priorities, work, projects and initiatives with the executive team's objectives that directly creates value. Strategy is implemented from the bottom to the top. Norton uses a fishing analogy to explain this: Strategy maps tell you where the fish are, but it is the projects, initiatives and core business processes that catch the fish.

DRIVER-BASED RESOURCE CAPACITY AND SPENDING PLANNING

For daily operations in which the normal, recurring work within business processes occurs, a future period's amount of product and service line volume and mix will never be identical to the past. In future periods, some customer-demand quantities will rise, and others will decline, which means that unless the existing capacity and dedicated skills are adjusted, you will have too much unnecessary capacity and not enough necessary capacity. These are dual problems. The former results in unused capacity expenses, whereas the latter results in missed sales opportunities or customer-infuriating delays due to capacity shortages. Both drag down profits.

Figure 11-3 illustrates advances in applying activity-based costing management (ABC/M) to minimise this planning problem. ABC/M principles solve operational budgeting by leveraging historical consumption rates to be used for calculating future period levels of capacity and spending.

Figure 11-3: (2) Recurring Expenses/Future Volume and Mix

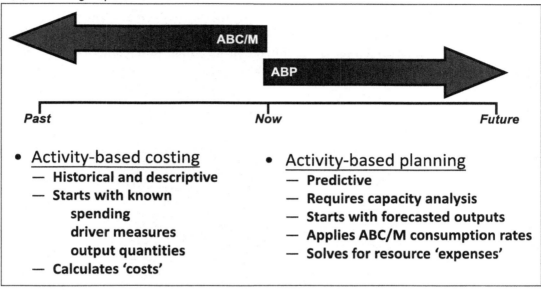

Source: Copyright Gary Cokins. Used with permission.

As an oversimplification, future spending is derived by calculating the ABC/M cost assignment network backwards. This was described in Part 4, Chapter 9, 'Predictive Accounting and Budgeting With Marginal Expense Analysis,' as closed loop activity-based planning and budgeting. The organisation starts by forecasting its activity-driver quantities (those were the actual driver quantities for past period costing). Then, it uses the calibrated activity driver unit level consumption rates from its historical costing to compute the amount of required work activities in the operational processes. Next, it equates these workloads into the number and types of employees and the needed non-labour-related spending.

This technique provides the correct, valid capacity and spending requirements. With this knowledge, management can intelligently intervene and approve adjustments by adding or removing capacity. It is a logical way of matching supply with demand. Once the capacity interventions (eg, employee headcount) and planned spending are approved, then a true and valid driver-based budget can be derived—not an incremental or decreased % change from last year—for each cost centre.

INCLUDING RISK MITIGATION WITH A RISK ASSESSMENT GRID

Measuring and managing risk possibilities identified in Part 3 is now transitioning from an intuitive art to more of a craft and science. Quantification with measures is needed; however, this area involves subjectivity and judgments. Therefore, each identified risk requires some form of ranking, such as by level of importance (high, medium and low). Because the importance of a risk event includes not just the impact but also the probability of occurrence, developing a risk assessment grid can be a superior method to quantify the risks and then collectively associate and rationalise all of them with a reasoned level of spending for risk mitigation. A risk map helps an organisation visualise all risks on a single page.

Figure 11-4 displays a risk assessment grid, with the vertical axis reflecting the magnitude of impact of the risk event occurring on the strategy implementation and the horizontal axis reflecting the probability of each risk event's occurrence. Individual risk events located on the map are inherent risks and are not yet selected for mitigation actions. That evaluation comes next. The risks located in the lower left area require periodic glances to monitor if the risk is growing, nominal to no risk mitigation spending. At the other extreme, risk events in the upper right area deserve risk mitigation spending with frequent monitoring.

Figure 11-4: (3) Risk Assessment Grid
... ERM is not just contingency planning

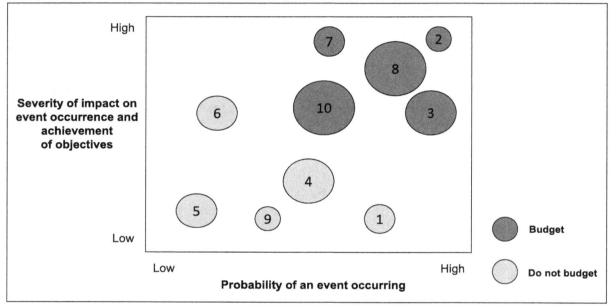

Source: Copyright Gary Cokins. Used with permission.

The risks in the risk assessment grid are evaluated for mitigation action. This grid reveals that risk numbers 2, 3, 7, 8 and 10 are in a critical zone. Management must decide if it can accept these five risks, considering their potential impact and likelihood. If not, management might choose to avoid whatever is creating the risk, for example, entering a new market. Some mitigation action might be considered, which would drive the risks to a more acceptable level in terms of impact and likelihood. As examples, an action might result in transferring some of the risk through a joint venture, or it might involve incurring additional expense through hedging.

Management must decide on the cost versus the benefits of the mitigation actions. Will the mitigation action, if pursued, move a risk event within the pre-defined risk appetite guidelines? Is the residual risk remaining after mitigation action acceptable? If not, what additional action can be taken? How much will that additional action cost, and what will be the potential benefits in terms of reducing impact and likelihood? After these decisions are made, then, risk mitigation actions can be budgeted, similar to the projects and initiatives derived from the strategy map.

FOUR TYPES OF BUDGET SPENDING: OPERATIONAL, CAPITAL, STRATEGIC AND RISK

Figure 11-5 illustrates a broad framework that begins with strategy formulation in the upper left and ends with financial budgeting and rolling forecasts in the bottom right. The elements involving accounting are shaded in green. Some budgets and rolling financial forecasts may distinguish the capital budget spending (#2 in the figure) from operational budget spending (#1), but rarely do organisations segregate the important strategic budget spending (#3) and risk budget spending (#4).

Figure 11-5: Linking Strategy and Risk to the Budget

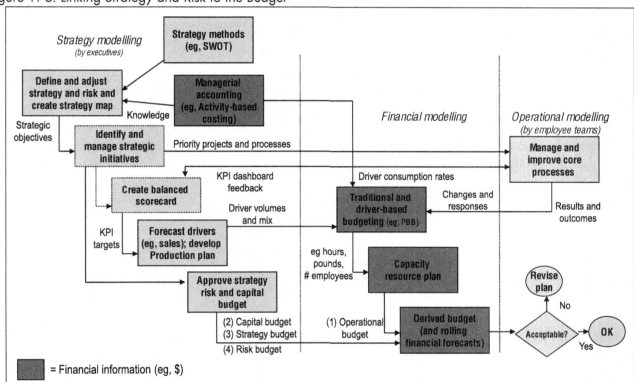

Source: Copyright Gary Cokins. Used with permission.

The main purpose of the figure is to illustrate that the budget depends on, and is derived from, two separate sources: a future demand-driven source (operational) and a project-based source (capital, strategic and risk mitigation).

The strategy creation in the upper left ideally uses meaningful managerial accounting information, such as understanding which products and customers are more or less profitable today and are potentially more valuable in the future. With this additional knowledge, the executives can determine which strategic objectives to focus on.

Note that the operational budget (#1)—those expenses required to continue with day-to-day repeatable processes—is calculated based on forecasted volume and mix of drivers of processes, such as the sales forecast, multiplied by planned consumption rates that are calibrated from past time periods (and ideally, with rates reflecting planned productivity gains). This demand-driven method contrasts with the often too primitive budgeting method of simply increasing the prior year's spending level by a few percentage points to allow for inflation. The operational budget spending level is a dependent variable based on demand, so it should be calculated that way.

Regardless of whether an organisation defines the strategic initiatives before or after setting the balanced scorecard's KPI targets, it is important to set aside strategy spending (#3) not much differently than budgeting for capital expenditures (#2). Too often, the strategy funding is not cleanly segregated anywhere in the budget or rolling financial forecasts. It is typically buried in an accounting ledger expense account. As a result, when financial performance inevitably falls short of expectations, it is the strategy projects' 'seed money' that gets deferred or eliminated. The priority must be reversed. Organisations must protect strategy spending and allow it to go forward because it is the key to competitive differentiation and successfully accomplishing the strategy.

The same goes for the risk mitigation expenses (#4). Enterprise risk management should be included in spending projections.

Note the question in the bottom right corner of Figure 11-5. Because the first pass at the 'derived' budget or rolling forecast will likely be unacceptably high and rejected by the executive team, the result is to adjust the plan. Hopefully, the project-based, strategy budget spending will be protected. As previously mentioned, organisations must protect strategy spending and allow it to go forward because it is a key to competitive differentiation and successfully accomplishing the strategy. This is similar to risk mitigation spending. Once the strategy and risk management spending are protected, the only other lever is to plan for productivity improvements in the consumption rates. This way, focused cost reductions (or future cost avoidance) become part of the EPM framework.

FROM A STATIC ANNUAL BUDGET TO ROLLING FINANCIAL FORECASTS

Most executive teams request frequent updates and revisions of the financial budget. These are referred to as *rolling financial forecasts* because the projection's planning horizon is usually well beyond the fiscal year-end date. Imagine if you were a CFO or financial controller required to re-process the budget quarterly (or even monthly) as a rolling forecast. There are not enough spreadsheets to do it! Only with computer automation that integrates several of the methodologies of the EPM framework, including good predictive analytics, can an organisation produce valid, derived rolling financial forecasts.

MANAGING STRATEGY IS LEARNABLE

Organisations with a formal strategy implementation process dramatically outperform organisations without formal processes. Building a core competency in strategy implementation creates a competitive advantage for commercial organisations and increases value for constituents of public sector organisations. Managing strategy is learnable. It is important to include and protect planned spending for strategic projects and initiatives in budgets and rolling financial forecasts. Those projects lead to long-term sustainable value creation.

Endnotes

1 Dr David Norton, Balanced Scorecard Collaborative
  Summit, November 7, 2006: San Diego, California.

2 Jones, Del. 'Turnover for CEOs is on record pace.'
  USA Today. July 12, 2006, p. 2B.

Part 5

INTEGRATING ENTERPRISE RISK MANAGEMENT AND ENTERPRISE PERFORMANCE MANAGEMENT

'No facts that are in themselves complex can be represented in fewer elements than they naturally possess. While it is not denied that many exceedingly complex methods are in use that yield no good results, it must still be recognized that there is a minimum of simplicity that cannot be further reduced without destroying the value of the whole fabric. The snare of the "simple system" is responsible for more inefficiency ... than is generally recognized.'
—Alexander H. Church
'Organization by Production Factors,' 1910

12

THE INTEGRATION OF ENTERPRISE RISK AND ENTERPRISE PERFORMANCE MANAGEMENT

Among businesses, there is increasing interest in the integration of enterprise risk management (ERM) and enterprise performance management (EPM), but there is confusion and lack of consensus about what each of them is, let alone how to integrate them. Finding the best way to apply meaningful measurements adds to the problem. Probably most disturbing is recent research that shows that no matter how interested in ERM and EPM they may be, executives are not adequately funding these functions, possibly due to fears that it will reduce profits. In addition, they are not allowing risk managers—or those whose function it is to assess risk—a seat at the executive table. Risk managers do play a valuable role within an organisation, however, by focusing on risk across the enterprise and mitigating the chance of potential risks to protect the organisation's profits.

An organisation needs both velocity with steering and control. The former comes from EPM (eg, strategy, key performance indicators [KPIs], alignment, customer profitability analysis, business intelligence, business analytics, rolling financial forecasts, etc) and the latter comes from ERM (eg, risk appetite statement, key risk indicators [KRIs], key control indicators, risk mitigation). Unrestricted EPM is dangerous without some limits. It is like driving too fast on a mountain highway with sharp turns. ERM is the accelerator and brake pedal while EPM steers to avoid a crash, hence, the steering and controlling. When EPM and ERM are combined, the organisation benefits by being better, faster, cheaper, and smarter (EPM) ... and safer (ERM).

HOW DO ERM AND EPM FIT TOGETHER?

EPM is much broader than its previously misperceived narrow definition of simply being dashboards and better financial reporting. EPM is a concept involving integrated methodologies. EPM is a part—albeit a crucial, integral part—of how an organisation realises its strategy to maximise its value to stakeholders, both in commercial and public sector organisations. This means that EPM must be encompassed by a broader overarching concept—enterprise risk-based performance management— that integrates with ERM.

Governance, risk and compliance (GRC) are important elements associated with EPM. From the EPM view described in this book, governance can be considered the stewardship of executives to behave in a responsible way, such as providing a safe work environment or formulating an effective strategy and compliance can be considered as operating under laws and regulations. Risk management, the third element of GRC, is the element most associated with enterprise performance management.

Governance and compliance awareness from government legislation, such as the Sarbanes-Oxley Act of 2002 and Basel II, is clearly on the minds of all executives. Accountability and responsibility can no longer be evaded. If executives err on compliance, they can go to jail. As a result, internal audit controls have been beefed up. (My personal opinion is today there is too much 'C' in GRC. Its substantial administrative effort has become a distraction for organisations to focus on organisational improvement.)

The 'R' in GRC has similar characteristics to EPM. The foundation for both ERM and EPM share two beliefs:

1. The less uncertainty there is about the future, the better.

2. If you cannot measure it, you cannot manage it.

IS RISK AN OPPORTUNITY OR HAZARD?

ERM is not about minimising an organisation's risk exposure. Quite the contrary, it is all about exploiting risk for maximum competitive advantage. A risky business strategy and plan always carries high prices. For example, when investment analysts are uncertain about a company's prospects, in part due to insufficient information, their inability to approximately predict financial results may lead to an analysis that will increase the firm's financing capital costs and, thus, reduce its stock price. Uncertainty can include uncertainty about accuracy, completeness, compliance and timeliness in addition to just being a prediction or estimate that can be applied to a target, baseline, historical actual (or average) or benchmark.

Effective risk management practices counter these examples by being comprehensive in recognising and evaluating all potential risks. Its goal is less volatility, greater predictability, fewer surprises and, arguably, most important, the ability to quickly bounce back after a risk event occurs.

A simple view of risk is that more things can happen than will happen. If businesses can devise probabilities of possible outcomes that are different from normal expectations, then they can consider creative options for how to deal with surprises and evaluate the consequences of incorrectly predicting outcomes. In short, risk management is about dealing in advance with the consequences of being wrong about a business decision.

However, as much as risks are potential hazards, they are also opportunities that can prove beneficial. For example, a rain shower may be a disaster for the county fair but creates a boon for an umbrella salesperson. Risk and opportunity are concerned with future events that may or may not happen. The events can be identified, but the magnitude of their effect is uncertain. However, the outcome of the events can be influenced with preparation in the form of ERM.

PROBLEMS QUANTIFYING RISK AND ITS CONSEQUENCES

Because of its potential for introducing new problems, risk is usually associated with new costs. In contrast, opportunity may lead to benefits, such as new economic value creation and increased turnovers. Most organisations cannot quantify their risk exposure—the potential for being affected by risk—and have no common basis to evaluate their risk appetite, or the amount of risk they are willing to absorb to generate the expected returns, relative to that exposure. The objective with ERM is not to eliminate all risk but, rather, to match risk exposure to risk appetite.

Not to be confused with contingency planning, ERM begins with a systematic method of recognising sources of uncertainty. It then applies quantitative methods to measure and assess three factors:

1. The probability of an event occurring
2. The event's severity of impact
3. Management's capability and effectiveness to respond to the event

Based on these factors, ERM identifies the triggers and drivers of risk, the KRIs, and then it evaluates alternative actions and associated costs to potentially mitigate, or take advantage of, each identified risk. These should ideally be included during the strategy formulation and re-planning processes, as well as reflected through financial projection scenarios, which are commonly called what-if analyses.

Multiple scenarios based on estimated probabilities of multiple variables are the accepted approach to glean impact sensitivities and determine which risk mitigation actions to pursue or reject. Using probabilistic scenarios provides strategists with distributions of possible outcomes and their source cause. Scenario analysis combines good business judgment with fact-based business analytics. Trend analysis, regression and correlation analysis are involved, but they no longer need to be scary memories of a university statistics course. Today, analytical software is designed for even the most casual user to perform these processes.

TYPES OF RISK CATEGORIES

With potentially hundreds of risks that may be identified, the task of dealing with them may seem daunting. Consequently, ERM can be better understood by categorising various risks. For example, identified risks could be grouped as being strategic, financial, operational or hazard. Or they could be grouped as external or internal and controllable or uncontrollable. Another example is financial or nonfinancial and insurable or noninsurable.

The following are six alternative risk categorisations:

1. *Price risk.* The risk that an increasing product or service offering supply or an aggressive price reduction from competitors will force lower prices and, consequently, profits.
2. *Market risk.* The risk that customer preferences and demand might quickly change. (For banking professionals, this is the risk from trading financial instruments.)
3. *Credit risk.* The risks of not meeting obligations, such as customers that fail to pay for their purchases, a mortgage holder that defaults on their loan or an entity that fails to settle a legal obligation.
4. *Operational risk.* The risk of loss resulting from inadequate or failed internal processes, people and technology or from external events.
5. *Strategic risk.* The risk of poor performance resulting from poor strategy selection and its implementation.
6. *Legal risk.* This can be a mixture of risks. There is the financial risk that banks refer to as liquidity risk from insufficient net positive cash flow or from exhausted capital equity-raising or cash-borrowing

capability. There is also risk from litigation (eg, in financial services, a lawsuit for losses due to poor financial advice) and from compliance violations with regulatory authority penalties.

Operational and strategic risks are the key risk types in which organisations can match their risk exposure to their risk appetite. They can wager both on formulating the strategy and, subsequently, on implementing the strategic objectives that comprise that strategy.

Operational risk, as previously defined, includes many possibilities, such as quality, workforce hiring and retention, supply chain, fraud, manager succession planning, catastrophic interruptions, technological innovations and competitor actions.

As earlier mentioned, operational risk management includes potential benefits from risks taken and from missed opportunities of risks not taken. Should we enter a market we are not now participating in? Should we offer an innovative product or service line offering while unsure of the size of the market or competitor reactions? How much should we rely on technology to automate a process? Will our suppliers dependably deliver materials or services at the right time or right quality? Organisations need to first measure their operational risk exposure and appetite in order to manage it.

Figure 12-1 illustrates aggregated quantitative risk measurement that guides balancing risk appetite with risk exposure.

Figure 12-1: Balancing Risk Exposure to Risk Appetite
The objective is not to eliminate all risk but, rather, to match risk exposure to risk appetite and tolerance.

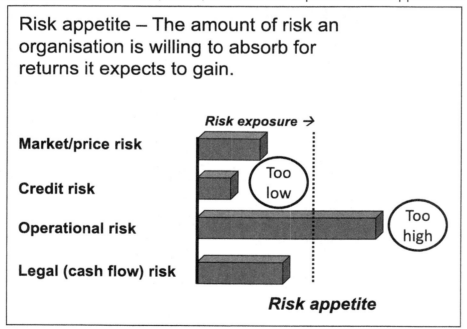

Source: Copyright Gary Cokins. Used with permission.

RISK-BASED EPM FRAMEWORK

The premise behind a risk-based EPM framework is to link risk performance to business performance. Whether defined narrowly or more broadly, EPM does not currently embrace risk governance, but it should. Risk and uncertainty are too critical and influential to omit. For example, reputational risk caused by fraud (eg, Tyco International), a terrifying product-related incident (eg, Johnson & Johnson's 1982 recall of Tylenol), or some other headline-grabbing event can substantially damage a company's market value.

Figure 12-2 illustrates how strategy formulation and implementation—risk management plus performance management—combine to achieve the ultimate mission of any organisation, which is to maximise stakeholder value. The risk-based EPM framework's four step sequence includes direction setting from the executive leadership (Where do we want to go?), as well as the use of a compass and navigation to answer the questions 'How will we get there?' and 'How well are we doing trying to get there?'

Figure 12-2: Risk-Based Enterprise Performance Management (assessment, context, alignment, controls, monitoring)

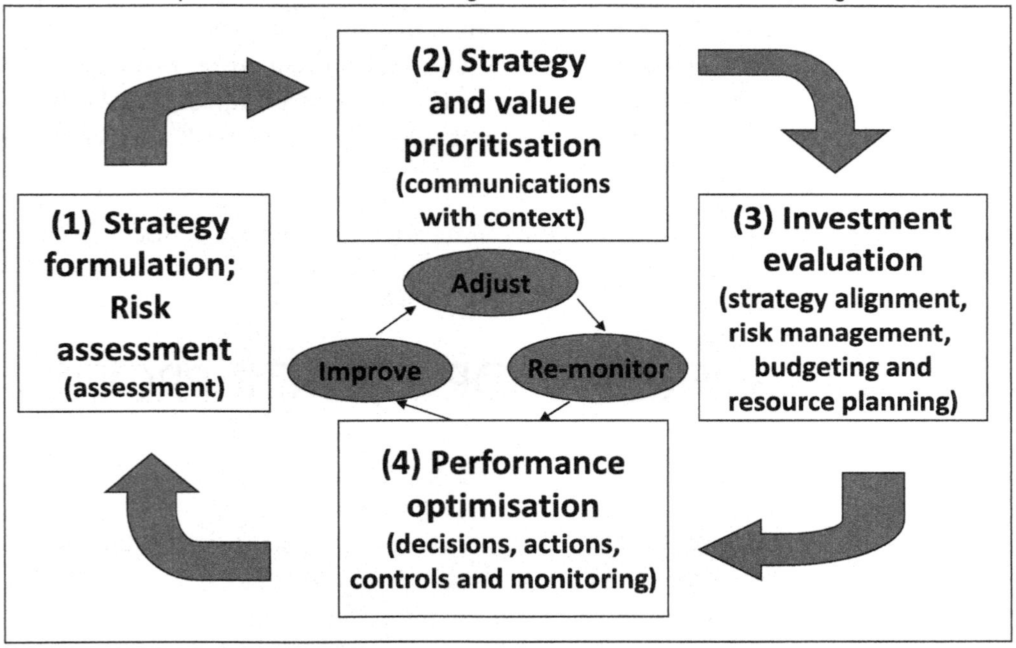

Source: Copyright Gary Cokins. Used with permission.

The four-step sequence is as follows:

Step 1: Strategy Formulation and Risk Assessment. In Step 1, the executives review and assess the key value drivers of their market and environment, a process that includes identifying KRIs, which is essential to understanding the root causes of risk. Identifying KRIs is a predictive process. The organisation can react before a future event occurs by continuously monitoring variances between expected and re-forecasted KRIs. The risk assessment grid described in Figure 11-4 is used in this step.

Step 2: Strategy and Value Prioritisation. A key component of EPM is formulated in step 2: the organisation's vision, mission and strategy map. Here the executives determine markets, products and customers to target. The vision, mission and strategy map is how the executive team both communicates to and also involves its managers and staff. The organisation then collectively identifies the vital few and manageable projects and selects the core processes at which to excel. Its actions are prioritised. This is also where research and development plus innovation projects are incubated.

Step 3: Investment Evaluation. A plan is one thing, but budgeting for how much to spend in order to accomplish the plan is another. The amount of investment is determined in step 3, and making that determination involves strategy implementation. Today's capital markets understand that customer value and shareholder value are not equivalent, nor are they positively correlated, but, rather, they have trade-offs with an optimum balance that companies strive to attain. This is why the annual budget and the inevitable rolling spending forecasts, typically disconnected from the executive team's strategy, must be linked to the strategy.

Step 4: Performance Optimisation. In step 4, all the execution components of the EPM portfolio of methodologies kick into gear. These include, but are not limited to, customer relation management, enterprise resource planning, supply chain management, activity-based cost management and Six Sigma and lean management initiatives. Because the organisation will have already identified its mission-critical projects and select core processes in step 3, balanced scorecard and dashboards, with their predefined KPIs, become the feedback mechanisms to steer the organisation in step 4. The balanced scorecard includes target versus actual KPI variance dashboard measures with drill-down analysis and colour-coded alert signals.The clockwise internal steps illustrated in Figure 12-2—Improve, Adjust, Re-Monitor—are how employees collaborate to continuously re-align their work efforts, priorities and resources to attain the strategic objectives defined in step 2.

The four steps are a continuous cycle in which risk is dynamically re-assessed and strategy subsequently adjusted.

RISK MANAGERS: FRIEND OR FOE OF PROFIT GROWTH?

Are risk managers supportive of long-term profit growth, or do they present obstacles that might stifle it? This topic unfortunately has recently taken a dark edge. A recent report of The Economist Intelligence Unit sponsored by The ACE Group, a global insurance company, and KPMG is titled, 'Fall guys: Risk management in the front line.' In the report, a risk manager claims he was fired for telling his company's board of directors that the organisation was taking on too much risk. Did management want to ignore a cautionary red flag to pursue higher profits? This involves whether strategy planners view risk managers as profit optimisers or detractors.

The Economist report was a result of extensive surveys and interviews, and the impact of the recent global financial sector meltdown was clearly on the minds of the respondents. The report highlighted that risk management and governance policies and structures require increased authority, visibility and independence. However, planned increases in investment and spending are modest or nonexistent, which is not a good sign. The reality is that the natural tension and conflict between the risk functions and the business' aspirations for higher profit growth remains present. The report's key findings are as follows:

- *Strategic risk management is in a relatively embryonic stage.* Executives view the identification of new and emerging risks as a key objective of risk management, but roughly two-thirds of them believe their organisation is weak at anticipating and measuring future risks.

- *Few organisations involve risk functions in key business decisions.* Few companies expect risk functions to play a part in strategic decision making in the near future.

- *Risk management should shift its emphasis from preventative activities to proactive and supporting ones.* Risk managers should expand beyond police-like controls and monitoring to also include identifying opportunities in order to achieve business objectives.

INVULNERABLE TODAY BUT AIMLESS TOMORROW

I continue to be intrigued by the fact that almost half of the roughly 25 companies that passed the rigorous tests to be listed in the once famous book by Tom Peters and Robert Waterman, *In Search of Excellence*, either no longer exist today, are in bankruptcy, or have poorly performed. What happened in the 25 years since the book was published? My theory is that once an organisation becomes quite successful, it becomes adverse to risk taking. Taking risks, albeit calculated risks, is essential for organisations to change and be innovative.

Classic managerial methods of past decades, such as total quality management, are now giving way to a trend of management by data. I would caution that extensively analysing historical data is not sufficient without complementing descriptive data with predictive information. The absence of reliable foresight explains why companies seem invulnerable one minute and aimless the next. An important competence that will be key to an organisation's performance is a combination of forecasting and risk management.

Endnotes

1 See www.businessresearch.eiu.com/fall-guys.html.

Part 6

BUSINESS ANALYTICS FOR ACCOUNTING AND FINANCE

'A new scientific truth does not triumph by convincing its opponents and making them see the light, but rather because its opponents eventually die out, and a new generation grows up that is familiar with it.'
—Max Planck, physicist and originator of the Quantum Theory, in *The Philosophy of Physics* (1936)

13

WHAT WILL BE THE NEXT NEW MANAGEMENT BREAKTHROUGH?

Since the 1890s, there have arguably been only a few major management breakthroughs with several minor ones. What will be the next big thing in management that can differentiate leading organisations from also-rans lagging behind them? I suggest one possibility at the conclusion of this chapter.

THE HISTORY OF MANAGEMENT BREAKTHROUGHS

Where do we draw the line between major and minor management breakthroughs of innovative methodologies that can provide an organisation with a competitive edge? I'm not sure, so the following list likely describes a blend:

- *Frederick Winslow Taylor's scientific management.* In the 1890s, Taylor, the luminary of industrial engineers, pioneered methods to systematically organise work. His techniques helped make Henry Ford wealthy when Ford's car company applied these methods to divide labour into specialised skill sets in a sequential production line and set stop-watch measured time standards as target goals to monitor employee production rates. Production rates faster than the standard were good, and slower were bad. During the same period, Alexander Hamilton Church, an English accountant, designed a method of measuring cost accounting variances to measure the favourable and unfavourable cost impact of faster or slower production speeds compared to the expected standard cost.

- *Alfred P. Sloan's customer segmentation.* Henry Ford's pursuit of a low unit cost per a single type of car (ie, the Model T) was countered with an idea championed by Alfred P. Sloan, who became President of General Motors in 1923. Sloan advocated expansion of product diversity in style, quality and performance, with increasingly more expensive features in car models as a staircase for higher income consumers to climb, starting with the Chevrolet and ultimately peaking with the Cadillac. It revealed the power of branding to retain customer loyalty.

- *Harvard Business School's Alfred D. Chandler Jr.'s organisational structure.* In 1962, Professor Chandler's pathbreaking book, Strategy and Structure, concluded that a factor explaining why some large companies fail or succeed involved how they learn about customers and how they understand the boundaries of their competencies to focus their strengths.

- *Harvard Business School's Michael E. Porter's theories of competitive advantage.* It is hard to believe that prior to Porter's 1970 book, *Competitive Strategy: Techniques for Analyzing Industries and Competitors,* very few organisations had a formal strategic planning department. Today, they are commonplace. Conglomerates comprising many diverse businesses were becoming numerous in the 1960s when Porter introduced his 'four forces' approach for individual businesses to assess their strengths and opportunities. His message was strategy is about making tough choices.

- *Total quality management from Edward Deming, Joseph Juran and Phil Crosby.* The total quality management (TQM) and continuous quality improvement programmes of the 1970s were a response to Japanese manufacturers grabbing market share as they progressed from being viewed as making cheap products to high quality ones. During the same time period, Shigeo Shingo and Taiichi Ohno of Toyota Motors, introduced 'pull-based,' just-in-time (JIT) production systems that were counter to traditional, large batch-and-queue production management economic lot size thinking. JIT provides faster throughput with less inventories. In the 1990s, at Motorola Mikel, Harry introduced a TQM refinement called Six Sigma, which recently has merged with lean management techniques.

- *Michael Hammer's business process re-engineering.* In the early 1990s, Michael Hammer recognised the importance of focusing on and satisfying customers. He observed that stove-piped and self-serving organisational departments were inefficient at serving customers and that the best way to improve service, particularly given the rapid adoption of computers, was not to just modestly improve business processes but, rather, to radically re-engineer processes with re-design.

- *Pepper and Rogers' customer relationship management.* In 1994, Martha Rogers and Don Peppers authored the book, *Customer Relationship Management—One-to-One Marketing*, which announced the eventual death of mass selling and mass marketing. It described how computers could track characteristics and preferences of individual customers.

- *Peter Senghe and organisational learning.* Around 1980, Professor Peter Senghe of MIT, recognising that many industries were increasingly dependent on educated knowledge workers, published research that concluded a differentiator going forward between successful and unsuccessful organisations is the rate of organisational learning—not the amount, but the rate.

- *Kaplan & Norton's strategy maps and balanced scorecard.* In 1996, Professors Robert S. Kaplan and David Norton published the first of four related books, *The Balanced Scorecard.* They recognised that executives were failing not due to poor strategy formulation but, rather, failure to successfully implement it. They advocated executives to communicate their strategy to employees using visual maps and shifting performance measures from month-end financial results to non-financial operational measures that aligns work and priorities with the strategy.

WILL BUSINESS ANALYTICS BE THE NEXT BREAKTHROUGH?

Enterprise performance management (EPM), by applying its broad definition as the integration of multiple managerial customer, operational and financial methodologies, embraces all the preceding advances. EPM integrates methodologies and their supporting systems to produce synergy not present when they are implemented in isolation of each other.

Professor Tom Davenport of Babson College in Massachusetts and Accenture's Jeanne Harris have authored two books, *Competing on Analytics and Analytics at Work*. Their books propose that the next differentiator for competitive advantage will be business analytics. Their premises are that organisations need much deeper insights and that change at all levels has accelerated so much that reacting after the fact is too late and too risky. They assert that organisations must anticipate change to be proactive, and the primary way is through robust quantitative analysis. This is now feasible due to the combination of massive amounts of economically stored business intelligence and powerful statistical software that can provide previously undetected patterns and reliable forecasts.

For example, customers can be finely micro-segmented in multiple combinations, such as age, income level, residence location and purchase history, and patterns can be recognised that can predict which customers may defect to a competitor, providing time to attend to such customers with a deal, offer or higher service level to increase retention levels. As an additional example, minute shifts in customer demands for products or services can be real-time monitored and projected to speed or slow actions and spending to induce customer behaviour.

EPM is not just better at managing performance but at improving performance. Integrating systems and information is a pre-requisite step, but applying business analytics, especially predictive analytics, may be the critical element to achieve the full vision of EPM.

14

HOW DO BUSINESS INTELLIGENCE, BUSINESS ANALYTICS AND ENTERPRISE PERFORMANCE MANAGEMENT FIT TOGETHER?

The late Nobel Prize-winning nuclear physicist Richard Feynman learned a valuable lesson as a child. His father showed him a picture of a bird species and told Feynman its name in several different languages. Then his father noted that regardless of the bird's various names, it did not in any way affect the reality of the bird's existence or its physical features. The lesson for Feynman was that no matter what name people use for something, it does not alter what that something is. We can apply that lesson to the confusion today about the difference between mainstream business intelligence (BI),[1] business analytics (BA) and enterprise performance management (EPM).

Are BI, BA and EPM different words for the same species or two different species ... or animals? Are BI and BA part of EPM? Or is EPM part of BI and BA?

It is an ambiguous question because the underlying inputs, processes, outputs and outcomes of an organisation, whether a public sector government agency or a commercial business, may arguably have some parts that belong to BI and BA, whereas others belong to EPM. The key word in that sentence is *arguably*. This argument arises because IT-centric people often see an enterprise as a ravenous consumer of billions of bytes of data intended to manage the business (a BI view). In contrast, leaders, managers and employee teams typically view the same enterprise as an organism with a purpose and mission (an EPM view). They desire solutions and applications that achieve results. How can BI and BA be reconciled with EPM? The enterprise is like that single species of bird—nothing can change its existence in reality.

THE RELATIONSHIP BETWEEN BUSINESS INTELLIGENCE, BUSINESS ANALYTICS AND ENTERPRISE PERFORMANCE MANAGEMENT

EPM puts BI into context. BI reporting consumes stored data that first must be cleansed and integrated from disparate source systems and then transformed into information. Analytics produces new information. EPM then leverages and deploys the information. EPM requires BI as a foundation. When analytics are added to BI and EPM, organisations gain insights for better and timelier decision making. That is, in this context, information is much more valuable than data points because integrating and transforming data using calculations and pattern discovery results in potentially meaningful information that can be used for decisions.

The greater the integration of the EPM methodologies and their various types of analytics, especially predictive analytics, the greater the power of EPM. Predictive analytics are important because organisations are shifting from managing by control and reacting to after-the-fact data, to managing with anticipatory planning, so they can be proactive and make adjustments before problems arise.

For example, a car manufacturer's warranty claims can be globally analysed to detect a design problem. In another instance, the history of an individual's credit card purchase transaction data can be converted to information that, in turn, can be used for decisions by retailers to better serve the customer or provide customised offers to sell more to them.

A survey by the global technology consulting firm Accenture reported that senior U.S. executives are increasingly more disenchanted with their analytic and BI capabilities.[2] Although they acknowledged that their BI (regardless of how they personally define it) provides a display of data in terms of reporting, querying, searching and visual dashboards, they felt their mainstream BI still fell short. An organisation's interest is not just to monitor the dials, it is, more importantly, to move the dials. That is, just reporting information does equate to managing for better results, but what is needed are actions and decisions to improve the organisation's performance. Having mainstream BI capability is definitely important, however, it often comes about as the result of departments needing advances that their IT function could not provide. Extending BI across the organisation so that mini-BI applications can talk is a mission-critical differentiator for organisational success and competitiveness.

Managing and improving are not the same things. Improving is how an organisation wins. To differentiate BI and BA from EPM, EPM can be viewed as deploying the power of BI and BA, but all three are inseparable. Think of EPM as an application of BI. EPM adds context and direction for BI. For example, in physics, BI is like potential energy, whereas BA and EPM is the conversion of potential energy into kinetic energy. Coal, when heated, provides power to move things. To use a track and field analogy, BI is like the muscle of a pole vaulter, and BA and EPM is that same athlete clearing higher heights. BI is an enterprise information platform for querying, reporting and much more, making it the foundation for effective performance management. BA and EPM drive the strategy and leverage all the processes, methodologies, measurements and systems that monitor, manage and, most importantly, improve enterprise performance. Together, BI, BA and EPM form the bridge that connects data to decisions.

With EPM, the strategy spurs the application of technology, methodologies and software. As methodologies, which are typically implemented or operated in isolation of each other, are integrated, the strength and power of BA and EPM grow. Technologies, such as software, support the methodologies. Software is an essential enabler, but the critical part is in the thinking. That is, one must understand the assumptions used in configuring commercial software and, more importantly, have a vision of the emerging possibilities to apply the new knowledge that BI, BA and EPM produces.

OVERCOMING BARRIERS

Many organisations have already begun with basic levels of EPM. Their challenge now is to move up to higher stages of maturity that include integrating EPM's methodologies and imbedding analytics into them. A key consideration to expanding an organisation's journey is to recognise that the barriers and obstacles are no longer technical ones, but rather social and cultural. These include human nature's resistance to change, fear of being measured and held accountable and weak leadership. Hence, behavioural change management is a key to realising value from EPM. A consideration for the executive team is to create a culture for measurements and analytics and to remove any fear that employees have of reprisals from what is discovered.

Like the bird that Feynman's father described, we should not waste valuable energy debating BI versus BA versus EPM—we may get caught up in semantics. Rather, we should progress to where BA and EPM deploy the power in BI with its enterprise information platform so that organisations can advance from managing to improving.

Endnotes

1 The IT community distinguishes between 'little'
business intelligence for query and reporting and
'big' business intelligence for the platform where
information is stored and managed. This chapter's
emphasis is on the latter.

2 2005 News Release, 'Companies Need to Improve
Business Intelligence Capabilities to Drive Growth,
Accenture Study Finds,' www.Accenture.com.

15

CFO TRENDS WITH ANALYTICS

A managerial movement that is now happening and gaining in popularity is the application of business analytics for organisations, which helps them gain insights so they can make good decisions and decide the best actions to take. This topic was once the domain of quantitative analysts and statistical geeks developing models in their cubicles. Today applying analytical methods is on the verge of becoming mainstream.

Which line management function may be in the best position to endorse and drive the adoption of business analytics? Is it marketing, operations or sales? Might it be the finance and accounting function? They already have a propensity for quantitative analysis. It is in their DNA.

One way to draw my conclusion about this emerging movement is to listen to the chatter and debate about the topic. Articles in IT magazines and on websites about 'Big Data' and the need for analytics of all flavours, such as segmentation analysis, are increasingly prominent. Debate is always healthy. Some IT analysts view applying analytics as a fad or being way overvalued. Others, such as leading proponents of analytics like authors Tom Davenport of Babson College in Massachusetts and Jeanne Harris of Accenture, claim that an organisation's achievement of competencies with analytics will provide a competitive edge.

Predictive analytics is one type of analytical method that is getting much attention because senior executives appear to be shifting away from a command-and-control style of management—reacting after the fact to results—to a much more anticipatory style of managing. With predictive analytics executives, managers and employee teams can see the future coming at them, such as the volume and mix of demands to be placed on them. As a result they can adjust their resource capacity levels and types, such as the number of employees needed or spending amounts. They can also quickly address small problems before they become big ones. They can transform their mountains of raw data into information to test hypothesis, see trends and make better decisions.

ANALYTICS AS THE ONLY SUSTAINABLE COMPETITIVE ADVANTAGE

For the last few decades many executives and strategic consulting firms have followed the framework of the popular Harvard Business School professor Michael S. Porter. Porter's writings include three types of generic strategies, discussed as follows. Notice that with today's technology-driven markets and economies, each generic strategy is vulnerable:

1. *Cost leadership strategy*. This is accomplished by improving process efficiencies, unique access to low-cost inputs (eg, labour, materials), vertical integration, or by avoiding certain costs. However today other firms using lean management techniques and data analysis methods can quickly lower their costs.

2. *Differentiation strategy*. This is accomplished by developing products or services, or both, with unique traits valued by customers. However today there can be imitation or replication of products and services by competitors (eg, smart phones) or changes in customer tastes.

3. *Focus strategy*. This is accomplished by concentrating on a narrow customer segment with entrenched customer loyalty. However today broad market cost leaders or micro-segmenters can invade a supplier's space and erode its customers' loyalty.

So how will an organisation gain a competitive edge? In my opinion the best defence is agility, with quicker and smarter decision making. This is accomplished by achieving competency with business analytics that can provide a long-term, sustaining competitive advantage. It means creating an organisational culture for metrics and analytics.

RESISTANCE TO CHANGE AND PRESUMPTIONS OF EXISTING CAPABILITIES

Some organisations may believe because they hired or trained employees with analytical skills that they have fulfilled the need to be analytical. However there are misconceptions about what analytics really is. To demonstrate this, the following is a true experience of one of my work colleagues.

A large department store retailer accepted a brief meeting with my co-worker for possible clarification about how analytics can increase profit lift from individual customers. The company's president, chief marketing officer and head of customer analytics attended. They were somewhat impatient because they were confident they already had an effective programme in place because many of their customers used a loyalty card at the checkout counter.

My colleague described that with access to each customer's profile (eg, age, address, gender etc) and their purchase history, a real-time analytics system could substantially increase the probability that a customer will actually respond to an offer, deal or intervention—and when. The first answer comes from data mining and the latter from forecasting—two of the many components of business analytics.

After the brief presentation with only a few minutes of the scheduled meeting left, the head of customer analytics concluded that the company was already using appropriate techniques. My co-worker then took a risk. The day prior to the meeting he went to one of the retailer's stores and purchased a travel-size shampoo and toothpaste using his loyalty card. He repeated the identical purchase a second time. In the meeting he placed both receipts on the table and turned them over. One receipt had a discount offer for a feminine hygiene product. The other receipt's discount was for cat food. My colleague, a male, has no pet. The chief marketing officer asked the head of customer analytics for an explanation. The answer was that 'those were among the hundred high-profit-margin products that are being promoted this month.'

In this example, there was no true connection to the individual customer, and the checkout register did not have sufficient technology to quickly access in real time customer-specific deals. The three executives had a kind of epiphany. They are now piloting a store entrance kiosk where customers can swipe their loyalty cards and receive personalised discounts and offers.

The kiosk substantially improves sales compared to the checkout register method. What I omitted from this example is how the kiosk knows what specific discount or deal to offer. That requires statistical analysis of different customer behaviours (eg, an online retailer's feature showing 'Others who bought what's in your shopping cart also bought X'). Early results from the retailer's pilot kiosk programme were substantial. For the checkout register receipt, a 1.8% response rate was the norm. The response rate rose to 30% for the real-time store entry kiosk.

The intended point here is that applying statistical analysis, data mining and forecasting with a goal of optimisation is now in reach—and some organisations that may think they are applying these methods are only just starting to develop them.

It may be that the ultimate sustainable business strategy is to foster analytical competency among an organisation's work force. Today managers and employee teams do not need a doctorate degree in statistics to investigate data and gain insights. Commercial software tools are designed for the casual user. The accounting and finance function can lead this business analytics movement. However improvement in their skills and competencies will be needed.

EVIDENCE OF DEFICIENT USE OF BUSINESS ANALYTICS IN FINANCE AND ACCOUNTING

Research[1] by the publisher CFO.com reported deficiencies in current uses of analytics in finance. Roughly half of the 231 companies surveyed reported being less than 'very effective' at incorporating information for strategic and operational decision making purposes. Thirty-six percent of the respondents identified management intuition and experience as the primary decision criteria when making strategic and operating decisions. Only 17% said that statistical analysis and modelling are primary decision criteria, and the largest number of respondents (36%) reported that their companies make 'little or no use' of more sophisticated techniques.

Fifty-three percent of the respondents said that robust modelling and analytics should play a greater role in their organisation's decision making. Finance executives appear willing to make the kind of investment needed to improve their ability to access and analyse business performance information. Seventy-six percent of the respondents anticipated that their companies will make at least a moderate investment in linking operational data to financial results.

Research by the IBM Institute for Business Value,[2] reports that the group of surveyed finance functions that demonstrate the highest effectiveness across the entire CFO agenda excels at two capabilities: finance efficiency brought about by process and data consistency, which helps unlock the power of analytics, and business insight to drive enterprise performance. Note the reference to the power of analytics. The study also states that this same group consistently applied five transformation enablers throughout their journey. These are addressing technology, enabling a sequential adoption of standard processes, using new operating models, applying better analytics and improving workforce efficiency. Again note the reference to applying better analytics.

The message from these two studies is clear. Analytics is playing an increasingly more important role with the CFO function. Analytics comes in many flavours, including, but not limited to, segmentation, correlation, regression and probabilistic analysis.

SOBERING INDICATION OF THE ADVANCES STILL NEEDED BY THE CFO FUNCTION

Another research study by The Data Warehouse Institute[3] states that 'finance can be a powerful agent of organizational change. It can leverage the information that it collects to assist executives and line of business managers to optimize processes, achieve goals, avert problems, and make decisions.' The study goes on to say

> forward-thinking finance departments have figured out how to transform themselves from back-office bookkeepers to strategic advisors.They have learned to partner with the IT department—more specifically, the business intelligence (BI) team—whose job is to manage information and deliver a single version of corporate truth. In so doing, they have liberated themselves from manual data collection and report production processes so they can engage in more value-added activities.

The research study further states that the finance function should be empowered to explore data on their own without IT assistance and that 'armed with analytical insights, the finance department can collaborate with business managers to optimize pricing, reduce inventory, streamline procurement, or improve product profitability. They can help business managers evaluate options, such as whether to add more salespeople, change commission fees, partner with a new supplier, or change merchandising assortments.'

The study makes a sobering statement by saying

> Unfortunately, the majority of finance departments have yet to adopt this new role to a significant degree. Our survey shows that although the finance department has made strides toward becoming a trusted partner with the business, it still has a long way to go. Less than half of financial professionals who responded to the survey believe their finance department, to a high degree, helps the organisation 'achieve its objectives' (41%), 'refine strategies' (35%), 'drive sales' (29%), or 'optimise processes' (29%). In fact, more than 20% of finance professionals gave their finance teams a low rating in these areas, with a larger percentage saying in effect that the finance department does little or nothing to help the business 'optimise processes' (43%) or 'understand and help drive sales' (50%).

MOVING FROM ASPIRATIONS TO PRACTICE WITH ANALYTICS

A problem with the research studies referenced is that they describe what the CFO function could be doing with analytics, with some blunt survey results describing the sizeable gap from the possibilities. However they do not provide tangible examples of the vision. Let's consider a few.

Customer Profitability Analysis to Take Actions

A trend for customers is to increasingly view suppliers' products and standard service lines as commodities. As a result, what customers now seek from suppliers are special services, ideas, innovation and thought leadership. Many suppliers have actively shifted their sales and marketing functions from being product-centric to customer-centric through the use of data mining and business intelligence[4] tools to understand their customers' behaviour — their preferences, purchasing habits and customer affinity groups. In some companies, the accounting function has supported this shift by reporting customer profitability information (including product gross profit margins) using the activity-based cost management principles described in Part 2. However, is this enough?

It is progressive for the accounting function to provide marketing and sales with reliable and accurate visibility of which customers are more and less profitable. Their company can also see why by observing the visibility and transparency of the internal process and activity costs that yield each customer's contribution profit margin layers. Often, sales and marketing people are surprised to discover that due to special services, their largest customers in sales are not their most profitable ones and that a larger subset of customers than believed are only marginally profitable—or worse yet, unprofitable. However a ranking of profit—from highest to lowest—of each customer does not provide all the information about why. This ranking is illustrated in Figure 15-1. It is a start but without giving all the answers. This is where data mining and analytical techniques can answer the 'why and so what' questions.

The use of ABC data leads to activity-based management (ABM). There are some low-hanging fruit insights from ABC data. For example, one can see relative magnitudes of activity costs consumed among customers. There is also visibility into the quantity of activity drivers, such as the number of deliveries that cause activity costs to be high or low. However this does not provide sufficient insight to differentiate relatively high profitable customers from lower-profit or unprofitable customers.

Figure 15-1: Why Are Some Customers More Profitable Than Others?

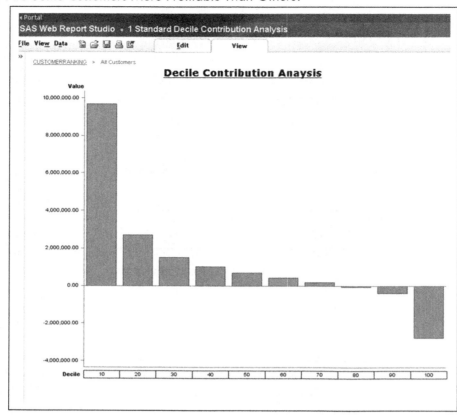

Source: Created with SAS software. Copyright 2010, SAS Institute Inc., Cary, NC, USA. All Rights Reserved. Reproduced with permission of SAS Institute Inc., Cary, NC.

One can speculate what the differentiating characteristics or traits might be, such as a customer's sales magnitude or location, but hypothesising (although an important analytics practice) can be time consuming. In attempting to identify the differentiating traits between more and less profitable customers, the major traits may not be intuitively obvious to an analyst. A more progressive technique is to use data mining and advanced statistical analytics techniques. This involves the use of segmentation analysis based on techniques involving decision trees and recursive partitioning. These techniques can give the sales and marketing functions insights into what actions, deals, services, offers, unbundled pricing and other decisions can elicit profit lift from customers.

The goal is to accelerate the identification of the differentiating drivers so that actions or interventions can be made to achieve that high-payback profit lift from varying types of customers. Analysts using ABC/M have benefited from applying online analytical processing multi-dimensional cubes to sort data. Even greater benefits and better decisions can come from applying data mining and advanced analytics.

Rationalising and Validating Key Performance Indicators in a Strategy Map and Balanced Scorecard

How do executives expect to realise their strategic objectives if all they look at is financial results like product profit margins; returns on equity; earnings and interest before interest, taxes, depreciation and amortisation

(EBITDA); cash flow and other financial measurements? These are really not goals—they are results. They are consequences. As previously mentioned, measurements are not just about monitoring the summary dials of a balanced scorecard. They are about moving the dials of the operational dashboards that actually move the strategic balanced scorecard dials.

Worse yet, when measures are displayed in isolation of each other rather than with a chain of cause and effect linkages, then one cannot analyse how much influencing measures affect influenced measures. This is more than just leading indicators and lagging indicators. It is timing relationships. As described in Part 3, Chapter 7, 'The Promise and Perils of the Balanced Scorecard,' a balanced scorecard reports the causal linkages, and its key performance indicators (KPIs) should be derived from a strategy map. Any strategic measurement system that fails to start with a strategy map or reports measures in isolation, or both, is like a kite without a string. There is no steering or controlling.

In Chapter 7 we learned that the strategy map's companion scorecard, on its surface, serves more as a feedback mechanism to allow everyone in the organisation, from front-line workers up to the executive team, to answer the question: 'How are we doing on what is important?' More importantly, the scorecard should facilitate analysis to also know why.

To go one step further, a truly complete scorecard system should have business analytics embedded in it. An obvious example would be correlation analysis to evaluate which influencing measures have what degree of explanatory contribution to influenced measures. Imagine a balanced scorecard's strategy map in which the thickness of the KPI arrow reflects the degree of explanatory contribution. That is how analytics embedded in a methodology brings more value. With KPI and PI correlation analysis, scorecards and dashboards become like a laboratory to truly optimise size and complexity. Consider that the thicker arrows (ie, higher correlation) could mean to provide greater budget funding because those levers appear to drive higher results of other KPIs.

MOVING FROM POSSIBILITIES TO PROBABILITIES WITH ANALYTICS

What could possibly affect an organisation's performance results? At the operational level, sales order volume could be up or down. Prices of purchased commodity materials like steel or coffee could be up or down. On a strategic macroeconomic level, consumer demand could be up or down. From a risk management perspective, weather fluctuations could adversely affect the best laid plans.

How could you know the impact, including the financial impact, since these ranges of possibilities occur at various levels? There are three broad ways: a single best guess; the worst, baseline and best likely outcomes; and a probabilistic scenario of the full range of outcomes. They all include predictions with analytics.

1. *Single Best Guess.* Most organisations plan for results based on their manager's best assumptions of what they estimate. For example, in the annual budgeting exercise, managers forecast sales mix volume, labour rates and prices of purchases. Each is a single point estimate, and the accountants aggregate them to produce a single budget.

2. *Worst, Baseline and Best Likely Outcomes.* The more advanced organisations consider three ranges of outcomes: worst, baseline and best likely outcomes. Separate predictions are made for the key variables

in the plan. Then the three overall possibilities are calculated. This provides a sense of the range of outcomes. These organisations might individually test the sensitivity of the key variables by increasing or decreasing each of them—one at a time—to see the effect and outcome.

3. *Multiple Probabilistic Scenarios.* The most advanced organisations take this process to its ultimate limit, from three scenarios to the full range of possibilities. That is, they estimate the probability distribution of each variable, perhaps as percentage increments from the base (eg, –20%, –10, 0% base, +10%, +20%). By combining these, they move from the three single point outcomes to viewing a distribution curve of dozens and, conceivably, hundreds or thousands of outcomes. The benefit is they can have more certainty of the increasingly uncertain world they operate in. In addition, the variables become understood as drivers of the results in which the level of each one may be able to be proactively managed in advance of their occurrence. These three levels are illustrated in Figure 15-2.

Figure 15-2: Analytics: Probabilistic Planning Scenarios

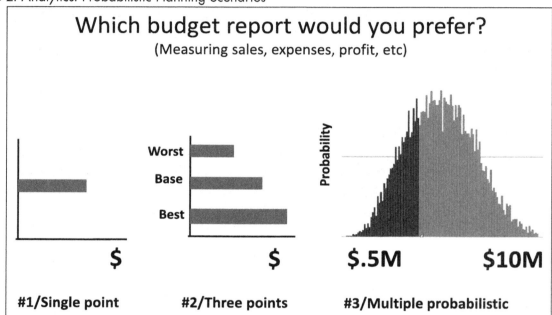

Source: Copyright Gary Cokins. Used with permission.

The breadth and granularity of the distribution curve increases as the probability ranges for each variable is segmented, as more variables (not just the key ones) are added, and as each variable is sub-divided (eg, from a product family to its individual products). The three-scenario approach gives a limited view of risk in contrast to the multiple probabilistic distribution curve. With the latter, sensitivity analysis can become very refined, including automated increases and decreases of each variable to determine which variable drivers have more impact.

Now take this process to an even higher level by increasing the time interval frequency of re-forecasting one or more (or even all) of the variable drivers.

What influences the accuracy and quality of the distribution curve? A critical one is the forecasting of each variable. If the baseline is really far off, then incrementing it up or down is also going to include error.

Achieving this best practices approach requires a combination of advanced analytics, reliable forecasting techniques (eg, Monte Carlo methods) and a powerful computational software engine. If this is supplemented with robust reporting, visualisation and analytical power, then it is nirvana. The full range of probabilistic outcomes can be viewed and, at more frequent time intervals, approach near real time. The benefits are endless. Risk management becomes scientific. Rolling financial forecasts replace static and fixed-in-time annual budgets. Drivers can be proactively managed, such as supply chain logistics and inventory management.

Predictive analytics is becoming a hot term with enterprise performance management. With the opportunity to move from just discussing the possibilities to understanding the factors affecting an organisation and also taking actions based on the interdependent probabilities, is anyone surprised? The organisation shifts from possibility to probability—managed probability—of outcomes.

FILL IN THE BLANKS: WHICH X IS MOST LIKELY TO Y?

Business analytics allows organisations to make decisions and take actions they could not do (or do well) without the analytics capabilities. The finance function can assist its line managers and employee teams. Consider these examples:

Increased Employee Retention

Which of our employees will be the next most likely to resign and take a job with another company? By examining the traits and characteristics of employees who have voluntarily left (eg, age, time period between salary raises, % wage raise, years with the organisation, etc), business analytics can layer these patterns on the existing work force. The result is a rank order listing of employees most likely to leave and the reasons why. This allows managements' selective intervention.

Increased Customer Profitability

Which customer will generate the most profit based on our least effort? As just described, by understanding various types of customers with segmentation analysis with recursive partitioning based on data about them (and others like them), business analytics can answer how much can optimally be spent retaining, growing, winning back and acquiring the attractive micro-segment types of customers that are desired.

Increased Product Shelf Opportunity

Which product in a retail store chain can generate the most profit without carrying excess inventory but also not have periods of stock outs? By integrating sales forecasts with actual near real time point-of-sale checkout register data, business analytics can optimise distribution cost economics with dynamic pricing to optimise product availability with accelerated sales throughput to maximise profit margins. Mark-down prices of inventories to be abandoned can be optimised.

These are three examples of the contribution that business analytics can provide. How can an organisation determine which X is most likely to Y? Hundreds of other examples exist in which the goal is to maximise or optimise something. With business analytics, the best and correct decisions can be made, and organisational performance can be tightly controlled and continuously improved. Without business analytics, an organisation operates on intuition, and optimisation cannot even be in that organisation's vocabulary. The CFO function has the competencies involving quantitative analysis. It is in their nature.

THE CFO FUNCTION NEEDS TO PUSH THE ENVELOPE

Research by Ventana Research has confirmed that the gap between current and potential use of analytics remains wide. It reports that information technology should be a particular focus because most finance organisations are not using IT assets as intelligently as they could. In particular, the finance function often focuses only on efficiency and neglects opportunities to use IT to enhance their effectiveness. Finance functions have made considerable progress in addressing their basic information needs (referred to as *20th century reporting requirements*), but most are a long way from providing the more complete, next level of information that can be used to improve performance (their 21st century requirements).

The benchmark research of this study shows there is important information that employees could receive—or already do receive—that would improve their organisation's performance and help align its actions to strategy. Information deficits, combined with poorly designed processes, can severely limit how well all departments, including the finance function, do their jobs. The study's recommendations are that CFOs and senior finance department executives focus on these three areas:

- Push the envelope when it comes to management reporting. To improve performance, companies must link more operational and financial data, make information available sooner and provide a richer set of data, including leading indicators for the business unit and relevant information about competitors, suppliers and factors that drive demand for the company's products or services.

- Have a disciplined, sustained process in place to address information technology barriers, especially infrastructure complexity, and to enhance the use of enterprise resource planning (ERP) systems. Typically, these are the root causes of issues preventing finance organisations from improving process implementation and preventing the disconnections that obstruct better alignment of strategy and implementation.

- Assess where there are shortfalls in the people, process information and technology dimensions of key financial functions, then define a plan with specific objectives and timetables that addresses these shortfalls.

Pursuing the application of analytics is common sense. One could argue that this study omitted as a root cause barrier the natural resistance to change and preference for the status quo. Without analytics, insights and understanding for better decision making is limited.

Endnotes

1 *Gearing Up for Growth: Financial Analytic Capabilities for Changing Times.* CFO Research Services, May, 2011. *Changing Times* is published by CFO Publishing LLC.

2 *Journey to a Value Integrator,* IBM Institute for Business Value, www-935.ibm.com/services/us/gbs/thoughtleadership/ibv-journey-to-new-value-integrator.html.

3 *Transforming Finance: How CFOs Use Business Intelligence to Turn Finance from Record Keepers to Strategic Advisors.* The Data Warehouse Institute, First Quarter, 2010.

4 *Data mining* is the process of extracting patterns from large amounts of stored data by combining methods from statistics and database management systems. It is seen as an increasingly important tool to transform unprecedented quantities of digital data into meaningful information, nicknamed business intelligence, to give organisations an informational advantage. It is used in a wide range of profiling practices, such as marketing, surveillance, fraud detection and scientific discovery.

5 *Financial Performance Management in the 21st Century—A CFO's Agenda for Using IT to Align Strategy and Execution.* Ventana Research, 2007.

Part 7

HOW TO BEGIN IMPLEMENTING ENTERPRISE PERFORMANCE MANAGEMENT

'There are three classes of people: Those who see. Those who see when they are shown. Those who do not see.'
—Leonardo da Vinci (Florentine painter and inventor), *Note Books*, c. 1500

16

WHERE DO YOU BEGIN IMPLEMENTING ANALYTICS-BASED PERFORMANCE MANAGEMENT?

As organisations embrace the full vision of analytic-based enterprise performance management (EPM)—not just the narrow, financial definition of better budgeting, planning and control—they frequently ask, 'Where should we start?' Some may be eager to begin with a balanced scorecard, others by measuring channel and customer profitability. Still others want to redesign their core business processes.

In fact, there is no one-size-fits-all answer. It depends on which of the analytic-based EPM methodologies provides the fastest, significant return and gets the employee buy-in ball rolling.

As described at the beginning of this book, analytics-based EPM is not new. Organisations have been doing it for years, arguably, even before computers arrived on the scene. However the traditional version of analytic-based EPM involved an implicit management strategy that was followed up by measurements of customer service, sales and order-fulfilment functions. It did not seek to integrate the various components of analytics-based EPM or to develop proactive core processes. Today, organisations realise they must integrate methodologies and their supporting systems, visually display measurements and apply predictive analytics to their processes.

As organisations realise that analytics-based EPM is really much more about improving performance rather than just controlling and managing it, they begin asking when do we begin to take what we already do to a much higher level?

ACCEPT THAT ANALYTICS-BASED EPM IS ABOUT INTEGRATION AND SPEED

An organisation attains the full vision of analytics-based EPM when executive leaders quickly communicate their strategy to their managers and employees and are committed to providing continuous updates to their plans. This allows everyone to be in sync and without wasted effort. Speed matters in communications. Performance suffers when managers and employees must repeatedly react to unexpected changes. To realise maximum benefits, all the EPM methodologies, including strategy mapping, customer relationship management, Six Sigma, lean management and anticipatory capacity resource planning, must be robust, seamlessly integrated and in sync. Because some organisations already have several of these methodologies in place but not necessarily connected, the 'where to get started' question depends on key factors related to the organisation's current situation.

For example, if a reasonably sound ABC/M system already provides information on which specific combinations of products, services, channels and customers earn or lose profit, executives may want to focus next on successful execution of their strategy by applying a strategy map and its associated balanced scorecard. Failure to implement a well-formulated strategy is a major frustration that frequently prompts executives to pursue analytics-based EPM. On the other hand, if the executive team is receiving cost information that is incomplete or flawed and inaccurate because of distorting indirect expense allocations—for example, the team is receiving only product or service line profit reporting but not full-channel and customer-segment profitability reporting—executives may want to upgrade their management accounting system by applying activity-based costing principles.

Again, determining where to start to integrate an analytic-based EPM framework depends on the organisation's weaker links.

Any approach to analytics-based EPM begins with the attitudes of senior leaders. If they launch into analytics-based EPM with a bad attitude—seeking to expose and weed out underperformers—the progress will be slow. Employees will be fearful. EPM is not about punishment but about remedy. However it does involve a great deal of accountability from individuals for achieving desired results. Wise leaders see their role as setting direction and continuous re-direction, clearly communicating their ideas and empowering their managers and employee teams to determine the best methods for moving the organisation forward in the direction communicated by its leaders.

ASSUMING AN ENLIGHTENED LEADERSHIP TEAM, THEN WHAT?

Organisations will not make quick progress by focusing exclusively on one methodology, such as better forecasting, and taking a year or longer to implement those improvements. Competitors will beat you, or customers' expectations will outpace you. Multiple methodology improvements should simultaneously take place. An increasingly accepted best practice for such improvements is to apply the 'plan-do-check-act' cycle. Start with rapid prototyping, followed by iterative remodelling for all the relevant methodologies. Naysayers will argue that the organisation can handle only a few projects at a time, but they underestimate the capabilities of people to work together when they are being guided by leaders, not just managers.

Start small, but think big. With rapid prototyping techniques, an organisation makes mistakes early and often, not later, when it is more costly to make corrective changes. This do-it-quick approach accelerates learning and brings fast results that gain buy-in from employees who are naturally resistant to change. Resistance to change is human nature. Iterative remodelling continues to scale and expand each of the prototyped methodologies to become repeatable and reliable production systems. Analytic-based EPM is like the gear-teethed cogs in a machine: The more closely linked and better meshed the methodologies are during implementation, the faster the organisation moves forward. It helps organisations gain better traction and faster speed in the right direction. Software technologies are very relevant, but their purpose is to support all the methodologies. They are enablers, not solutions.

EMBRACE UNCERTAINTY WITH PREDICTIVE ANALYTICS

Managers and employee teams will gradually see and understand the big picture, including how all the methodologies fit together. Those in commercial organisations will realise that creating higher profits and increasing shareholder wealth is not a goal but a result. For those organisations, the true independent variable is finely managing the innovation-based research and development and marketing spending to focus on the types of customers to retain, grow, acquire and win back, as well as those types of customers to avoid wasting money on. Leaders in public sector government organisations may view funding as a scarce commodity. Therefore, they have a need to maximise outcomes by increasing output or improving service delivery without additional resources.

Executives are constantly on a quest for the next breakthrough in managerial innovation. My suggestion is to start by integrating and enhancing existing methodologies that have proved their worth. It is likely that the organisation is implementing most of these at some level of competence. However, integration deficiencies may exist in some areas, leading to time lags that cause excessive and costly reactions.

Successful organisations adapt by performing much deeper analysis, such as better and more granular customer segmentation, which helps to provide insight into all the elements being managed. They are leveraging business intelligence. These leaders integrate their methodologies and supporting systems for better decision making. Their next major task is to get in front of the wave, using predictive analytics to seize opportunities and to mitigate risk by making changes before the effects of a problem can occur. Predictive analytics may well be the next major competitive differentiator, separating successful from mediocre or failing organisations. The uncertainty of future demands or events should not be viewed as a curse but, rather, embraced as something organisations can tame with the powerful and proven probabilistic tools that already exist.

Start now—everywhere. Most organisations over-plan and under-execute. For organisations that have experienced recent upheaval, now is the time to regain some order. With a nurturing attitude from executive leaders who act more like coaches than bosses, and with accelerated learning by managers and employee teams, organisations can move forward to complete the full vision of analytics-based EPM.

17

A CALL TO ACTION—BUILDING A BUSINESS CASE

In this book you have probably detected a common theme—start integrating now, and don't postpone it. Most enterprise performance management (EPM) advocates are growing tired of nagging organisations to adopt EPM and are now wagging our finger at them to get them going. Why are we so passionate about this topic? One explanation is because advocates have observed organisations that have integrated EPM components enjoy tangible and sizeable benefits. On the flip side, we have witnessed organisations who continue to defer integrating suffer adverse consequences.

THE OBSESSION WITH ROI JUSTIFICATIONS

Of course, many of you are insisting, 'Name names who have failed. Tell me the return on investment (ROI) on EPM.' To introduce my answers, let's start with pondering the question 'How many of the original Standard and Poors (S&P) 500 list originally created in 1957 are on that list today?' The answer is 74, which is just 15%. Of those 74, only 12 have outperformed the S&P index average.[1] My belief is when it comes to considering whether to implement and integrate the various component methodologies that constitute the EPM framework, there actually are two choices. Do it or don't do it. Many organisations neglect the fact that the choice to *not* act, which means to continue with the status quo and perpetuate making decisions the way they currently are, is also a decision.

What about this need to prove that it is worth it to act by calculating an ROI for EPM? Consider how you would measure the impact of having better performance measures from a strategy map and balanced scorecard system to drive employee behaviour. Or consider how you would measure the impact of better decisions resulting from having more accurate and explanative information from an activity-based cost management (ABC/M) system. You will eventually conclude that the many parallel improvement and change initiatives that organisations pursue (eg, total quality management, business process engineering) are simultaneously occurring. As a result, it is nearly impossible to trace benefits, such as cost savings or future cost avoidance, directly back to any individual change program. This is like trying to make a broken egg whole again.

One step removed from this ROI measurement challenge is to measure the effect that better information, such as from using an ABC/M methodology, serves as an enabler to boost the effect of all these improvement programs. This further complicates quantifying the financial returns from the contribution of each change initiative program.

I am not big on making decisions based on faith, but some managerial concepts just seem to be correct, and completing the full vision of the EPM framework is one of them. Take action or don't take action. Both choices have an ROI, and with EPM, my belief is that the former is positive, and the latter is negative.

MANAGEMENT AND THE IT FUNCTION CAN BE OBSTACLES

Most organisations make the mistake of believing that implementing analytics-based EPM methodologies is 90% math and 10% organisational change management with employee behaviour alteration. In reality, it is the other way around—probably 10% math and 90% about people.

A problem all organisations suffer from is their imbalance from how much emphasis they should place on being smart rather than being healthy. What is needed to correct this imbalance? Right from the start, you have to think like a sociologist and, arguably, you need to be a psychologist too. People matter—a lot. Never underestimate the magnitude of resistance to change. It is natural for people to love the status quo.

When organisations begin applying one of the many methodologies that constitute the full suite of analytics-based EPM, I believe they need two plans: an implementation plan and a communication plan. The second plan is arguably much more important than the first. There are always advocates for a new project, but there are also naysayers. Knowing in advance who the naysayers are is critical to either winning them over or avoiding them.

A command-and-control style of management that tries to mandate change through force went out years ago. Today's employee is a knowledge worker. When the executive team proclaims, 'We are now going to shift direction and go this new way,' most managers fold their arms in resistance and silently say to themselves, 'Convince me.'

The trick to general management is integrating and balancing the quantitative and behavioural managerial approaches and styles. Today command-and-control style executives who prefer to leverage their workers' muscles, but not their brains, run into trouble. Ultimately, people get things done, not computers or machines, which are simply conduits for arriving at results. Most employees do not enjoy being micro-managed. The good performers are people and teams who manage themselves, given some direction and timely feedback. Management creates value and produces results by leveraging people. Analytics-based EPM is much more than dials and levers. It is about people.

An obstacle to organisational improvement and strategy implementation is that employees have not been granted sufficient decision rights to act on the conclusions they have derived from business analytics and fact-based explorations. Decision rights remain hoarded at the top of the organisation. Empowering employees with decision rights and analytical tools with which to reach those decisions is the key to organisational improvement.

Studies have shown that the two major barriers to effective strategy implementation are (1) not distributing decision rights downward into the layers of the organisation chart, and (2) poor cross-functional information flows. Contrary to common belief, removing these two barriers trumps reshaping the boxes and lines in the organisation chart and incentive systems. An iron law of economics states that the better the decisions, the better the results, hence, continuous organisational improvement will follow, financial or otherwise.

However, another obstacle exists. IT often acts as a wall between the data and its users. They first speculate that two or more things are related or that some underlying behaviour is driving a pattern to be seen in various data. They want a set of capabilities for investigation and discovery. They apply business intelligence and analytics as confirmation more than as a somewhat random exploration. This requires users to have easy and flexible access to data, the ability to manipulate the data and the software to support their processes.

There will need to be a shift from this face-to-face adversarial confrontation to a side-by-side collaborative relationship to remove this wall. Part of the problem is how IT and analysts view each other.

Analysts view IT as an obstructive and uncooperative gatekeeper of data. They view IT as not possessing the skills to convert that data into useful information. Experienced analysts view IT as typically trying to prevent robust analysis. Analysts view IT as bureaucrats, who manage a set of technologies and whose main goal is to keep the lights on.

In contrast, IT increasingly views users as competitors, who may solve problems, but don't have to operate the solutions—they just make it harder to better manage capacity costs by using too many IT resources. IT sees users as a risky group that has low regard for data governance and security.

Analysts need speed and agility to be reactive and proactive, which requires them to be closer to the data for analysis and better decision making. Both IT and its users will need to remove the wall and collaborate and compromise by better understanding and appreciating each other's changing roles.

IS EPM ART, CRAFT OR SCIENCE?

During a business trip to Rome, I had some weekend time to be a tourist. How can anyone not admire the incredible structural achievements of Italian sculptors, artists and architects? There are so many wonderful structures to appreciate, including the Pantheon, the Coliseum, the Spanish steps and all the wonderful piazzas. There are also many beautiful churches, including St. Peter's Basilica in the Vatican. The structure of these churches, including their tall columns and ornate decorations, is breathtaking. Inside each church I visited, as I gazed at the high ceilings, I asked myself this question: 'How much of this beauty built by people centuries before us was the result of art, craft or science?' Similarly, for today's organisations implementing the various component methodologies of the analytics-based EPM framework, how much is art, craft or science? Let's further discuss this question.

Balancing a Smart, as Well as a Healthy, Organisation

In Chapter 7 I described the Newtonian versus the Darwinian view of managing. Despite my Newtonian view (which is probably shared by a vast majority in business and IT) that an organisation is a big machine that simply needs more gears, pulleys and dials to better operate it, behavioural change management is also substantially important. As mentioned, that is why one has to be a psychologist and sociologist to successfully implement EPM. I realise there is also a Darwinian view, which believes that an organisation is like an organism, and we must acknowledge its sense-and-respond behaviour.

A Newtonian organisation relies on fact-based information to make it smarter. A Darwinian organisation relies on employee-centric programmes and policies for improving morale to make it healthier. A balance of the Newtonian and Darwinian management styles is needed to be both smart and healthy.

For the next few paragraphs, let's explore how science, in the form of business analytics, can be inserted into EPM methodologies to make it smarter.

The Power of Business Analytics

- If you are a retail merchandiser with many stores and consumer items, you can use predictive analytics to continuously replenish a dynamically optimal level of inventory without having too many items languishing on the shelves or any stock-out items.

- If you are a hardware manufacturer and your suppliers are late in delivering component parts creating a shortage, your customer service representatives can influence customers to change their order at the same time the order is being placed by offering them slightly different product configurations, with a small discount, that includes the parts you have in stock.

- If you are a consumer packaged-goods producer, you can run short-duration marketing campaigns, target and predict the desired sales mix volume and instantly harmonise your production levels to optimise costs.

- If you are a business-to-consumer service, such as a bank or telecommunications firm, you can analyse the purchase history and preferences of your customer micro-segments (and even of each customer). That information, combined with individual customer profitability information, can help you tailor service offerings to up-sell and cross-sell to customers to optimise future sales and profits.

- If you are a human resources manager seeking to increase employee retention, you could analyse the characteristics and traits of employees who have left your organisation. The variables might include their ages, the frequency and amount of their salary increases, their lengths of employment and dozens of others. You could then apply these patterns to your existing work force to predict and order a list of the next most likely employees to resign (plus their reasons) and potentially intervene to prevent their departures (for those valuable employees you wish to retain).

- If you are a CEO desiring to better select and align your most influential balanced scorecard's key performance indicators (KPIs), you could continuously test the degree of statistical correlation between the cause and effect leading to lagging KPIs. This way you can keep improving those KPIs and, accordingly, apply weights to influence and align your employees' behaviour with the strategic objectives.

THE FUTURE OF ANALYTICS-BASED EPM

In the 1890s Frederick Winslow Taylor, a luminary of industrial engineers, pioneered scientific management methods to systematically organise work. His techniques helped make Henry Ford wealthy when Ford's automobile company applied these methods to divide labour into specialised skill sets in a sequential production line and set stopwatch-measured time standards as target goals to monitor employee production rates. Production at rates faster than the standard was good, and slower was bad. During the same period, Alexander Hamilton Church, an English accountant, designed a method of measuring cost accounting variances to measure the favourable and unfavourable cost impact of faster or slower production speeds compared to the expected standard cost.

Since then, as outlined in Chapter 13, 'What Will Be the Next New Management Breakthrough,' management science has gradually continued to support better decision making and improve an enterprise's performance. However the time has come to escalate the application of management science by leveraging business analytics.

An organisation should be viewed as a broad series of ongoing laboratory experiments in order to refine its decision making. Managers at all levels should be formulating ideas and theories about what will best improve the organisation's performance. Based on these theories, the organisation should constantly test the effects of its actions for validation. Scientists, like biologists and astronomers, live by experimentation and test analysis. An organisation should, too, whether it is a commercial business or public sector government agency or ministry.

People are what it's all about, so I honour and respect the importance of applying the principles of behavioural change management. However my love for quantitative analysis influences me to conclude with a short narration by the great Princeton University mathematician and Nobel Prize winner, John Nash. Nash introduced a theory describing how rational human beings should behave if there is a conflict of interests. In the Academy Award winning movie about Nash's life, *A Beautiful Mind*, he said 'I like numbers because with numbers, truth and beauty are the same thing. You know you are getting somewhere when the equations start looking beautiful. And you know that the numbers are taking you closer to the secret of how things are.'

The executive management teams with the courage, will, caring attitude and leadership traits to take calculated risks and be decisive will likely be the initial adopters of fully integrated, analytics-based EPM systems and will achieve its full vision. Other executive management teams will follow them.

Endnotes

1 Presentation at the CFO Connections Conference
  by Professor Gary Biddle, University of Hong King;
  September 11, 2007, Beijing, China.

The information herein was adapted from:

Performance Management: Finding the Missing Pieces to Close the Intelligence Gap, Copyright © 2004 by John Wiley and Sons. Describing the full vision of performance management and how to reap the most benefits from it, *Performance Management* shows organisations how to use PM tools that have existed for decades or have become recently popular—such as balanced scorecards, Six Sigma and activity-based management—to collect data, transform and model the data into information, and Web-report it to users. Cokins exposes PM as not just an integrated set of improvement methodologies but also as a discipline intended to maintain a view of the larger picture and to understand how an organisation works as a whole. PM can be successfully applied to managing any organisation, including businesses, hospitals, universities, government agencies, military bodies and every other entity that has employees and partners with a purpose.

Performance Management: Integrating Strategy Execution, Methodologies, Risk and Analytics by Gary Cokins. Copyright © 2009 by John Wiley and Sons. Beginning with a tongue-in-cheek description of how not to pursue a performance management culture, this big-picture book clarifies what performance management really is, what it does, how it enables better decisions and how to make it work. Revealing the relevant aspects of performance management, it discusses why integration of multiple management methodologies and behavioural change management are crucial to overcome managers and employees' natural resistance to change.

These books can be purchased at bookstores and for more information on other management accounting products contact:

In the U.S.A.: American Institute of Certified Public Accountants (AICPA)
1211 Avenue of the Americas, New York, NY 10036-8775
USA Tel 888.777.7077
FAX 800.362.5066 www.aicpa.org
Visit the AICPA store at www.cpa2biz.com

In the United Kingdom: The Chartered Institute of Management Accountants (CIMA)
26 Chapter Street, London SW1P 4NP United Kingdom
Tel +44 (0)20.7663.5441
FAX +44 (0)20.7663.5442 www.cimaglobal.com

Two of the world's most prestigious accounting bodies, the AICPA and CIMA, have formed a joint-venture to establish the Chartered Global Management Accountant (CGMA) designation to elevate the profession of management accounting. The designation recognises the most talented and committed management accountants with the discipline and skill to drive strong business performance.

For more information on the CGMA designation, visit www.cgma.org or contact member services at:

In the U.S.A.: AICPA
220 Leigh Farm Road, Durham, NC 27707-8110
Email: service@aicpa.org
Tel.: 888 777 7077 (US toll free)
Tel.: + 1 919 490 4300 (international)

In the United Kingdom: CIMA
26 Chapter Street, London SW1P 4NP United Kingdom
Email: cima.contact@cimaglobal.com
Tel.: +44 (0)208 849 2251

CPSIA information can be obtained
at www.ICGtesting.com
Printed in the USA
BVOW04s1716020917
493700BV00010B/47/P